JEAN

T0166308

"He really formed .... *......mity.*
I learned how to do comedy from Jean Shepherd."

—JERRY SEINFELD

"What I got from him was a wonder at the world
one man could create.
I am as awed now by his achievement as I was then."

—RICHARD CORLISS, *TIME*

"Shepherd had the best influence on my sensibility. He
helped me pursue that sense of being different, being an
individual. He actually made me feel I wasn't alone."

BILLY COLLINS, U.S. POET LAUREATE

"I don't think any sense of humor is funny. Rarely.
Jean Shepherd is funny."

—ANDY KAUFMAN

"Shep had an extraordinary ability to tap into
the American psyche and communicate with an
audience of devoted fans and listeners."

—HARRY SHEARER 2-HOUR NPR SPECIAL

SHEP'S ARMY
Bummers, Blisters, & Boondoggles

Jean Shepherd

Foreword by
Keith Olbermann

Edited with an introduction by
Eugene B. Bergmann

SHEP'S ARMY

Published by Arrangement with the Estate of Jean Shepherd,
Irwin Zwilling, Executor
Copyright © 2013 OPUS
Introduction copyright © 2013 Eugene B. Bergmann
Foreword copyright © 2013 Keith Olbermann

AN OPUS TRADE PAPERBACK ORIGINAL

All rights reserved.

Printed in the United States of America.

No part of this book may be reproduced, or stored in a retrieval system, or
transmitted in any form or by any means, electronic, mechanical, photocopying,
recording, or otherwise, without express written permission of the publisher.

ISBN: 978-1-62316-012-8

Publisher's Cataloguing-in-Publication Data

Shepherd, Jean.

　　Shep's army : bummers, blisters, & boondoggles / Jean Shepherd ; foreword
by Keith Olbermann ; edited with an introduction by Eugene B. Bergmann. — New
York : Opus, c2013.
　　p. ; cm.
　　ISBN: 978-1-62316-012-8 (print) ; 978-1-62316-013-5 (epub) ; 978-1-
62316-014-2 (kindle) ; 978-1-62316-015-9 (Adobe PDF)
　　Includes bibliographical references.
　　Summary: Jean Shepherd, the great Amrican humorist, radio raconteur,
master storyteller, and bestselling author, has left his indelible imprint on American
culture. This collection of Jean Shepherd army stories was selected and transcribed
from radio programs by Shepherd biographer Eugene Bergmann and is in print for
the first time. — Publisher.
　　1. United States. Army — Military life — Anecdotes. 2. World War,
1939-1945 — Humor. 3. United States — Social life and customs — 20th
century — Fiction. 4. American wit and humor. 5. Humorous stories, American.
6. Autobiographical fiction. 7. Humorous fiction. 8. Radio programs. I. Bergmann,
Eugene B. II. Olbermann, Keith, 1959- III. Title.

PS3569.H3964 S54 2013
813.54 — dc23   1308

A Division of Subtext Inc., **A Glenn Young Company**
44 Tower Hill Loop • Tuxedo Park, NY 10987
Publicity: E-mail OPUSBOOKSPR@aol.com
Rights enquiries: E-mail GY@opusbookpublishers.com
All other enquiries: www.opusbookpublishers.com

OPUS is distributed to the trade by The Hal Leonard Publishing Group
Toll Free Sales: 800-524-4425
www.halleonard.com

For All the Members of Company K

"You don't see this kind of stuff in army movies."
—JEAN SHEPHERD

CONTENTS

PART FOUR: AN ARMY EDUCATION: INDEPENDENT STUDY

PART FIVE: MUSTERED OUT AT LAST!

APPENDIX

FOREWORD

by KEITH OLBERMANN

S hep apologized to my friend—and quickly.

"I didn't mean to snap, son." He sighed and drew a palm over his mouth. "It's just that I love the radio shows. But the books! I slave over the books! They have to be exactly right. Exactly!... Right!" Why he was opening up to a tenth-grader I'll never know (nor will my fellow tenth-grader—it happened to him, not me). But open he did.

"I know if I'll be remembered, I'll be remembered for the radio shows, not the books [the movie was still in the future]. I guess that's okay. But, see, the radio shows only have to make sense. The books are..." Jean Shepherd paused, and if he was doing so for emphasis it worked. My friend remembered the pause as he retold the story a decade later: "The books are forever!"

And they are.

When you read, when you laugh, when the seminal truths of the universe that come out of the sky and reveal themselves to the observant of the Midwest of 1937 or the Northeast of 2013 or the West of 2274 again peek through and make you shiver with their transcendent honesty and applicability, just remember Jean

Shepherd sweated his privates off to tell you these timeless facts, and to get the message exactly right—before the muse escaped his vision. Shep would have found these spirited transcriptions of his army stories also got it "exactly right"!

So shout "Excelsior!" at the nearest Fathead, and thank whatever deity you favor that this flawed man who couldn't resist yelling at one of his fifteen-year-old radio fans, existed for a time—"Just to tell thee…"

INTRODUCTION

Inducted into the army at age twenty, Shepherd served from July 1942 until December 1944, spending his entire time in the States. Thus, he has no tales of battlefield valor to tell, but he does tell some doozies about KP with four hundred dead chickens, USO hospitality with a Daisy Mae look-alike, and near death on a desolate field of telephone poles—and with that, you still ain't heard nothin' yet about his adventures on the home front.

Because he is so secretive about details of the real life he lived, the truth of what he did and where he did it is hard to come by. He sometimes speaks of being at Camp Crowder, Missouri, where indeed there was a large Signal Corps training facility. In more than one of his tales, he speaks of going into the nearby town of Neosho, Missouri, where, just as he fictionally alludes to it, families had the custom of inviting soldiers home for Sunday dinner. He appears to have spent much of his time in a semitropical environment near or in the Everglades. He frequently talks about the intense heat, the insects, and the tropical flora and fauna. This was the historical reality of Camp Murphy, a radar training base within an enlisted man's short bus ride to West Palm Beach, Florida, and the likely suspect.

Army inductees who were ham radio operators as was Shepherd were often automatically marshaled into the Signal Corps, the army unit responsible for communication. We know he was a capable Morse code operator from early adolescence, and through his army stories, he claims to have learned everything from climbing telephone poles to operating the new-fangled radar equipment. He sometimes claims to have been in a mess-kit repair company, whose insignia was mess kits with crossed forks on a background of SOS. (Anyone needing a definition of SOS should ask a soldier about creamed chipped beef on toast.)

Even though most of his tales are anchored in the Signal Corps, all are universal regarding what he sees as the military world. They depict what he saw of the lives of millions of GIs living a day-to-day reality of constraint, discomfort, and sometimes the wearing away of the polite veneer of civilized behavior. Millions of ordinary guys who never see the drama— the hell—of war up close, and therefore seldom have the opportunity to perform either bravely or cowardly, or even to carry on in the face of calamity, simply live, struggle, and survive the dehumanizing indignities of military life in a way that, for Shepherd, is seldom shown and always unsung. He believes that such experience has interest and value, especially because it is the reality for most of us most of the time. And he knows how to depict it with understanding and frequently with laugh-out-loud humor.

Surveying the audios of his available radio broadcasts gives added appreciation for his many armed services stories. They are very popular with both listeners and readers, but other than a few published decades ago they have not, until now, become available in print. We have only about fifteen hundred of the approximately five thousand broadcasts that have so far surfaced from which to select army stories to publish. One wonders what gems of broadcasts, and the gems of stories within them, have simply disappeared into the ether. Yet many glories survive. Exploring the available tapes, one finds tales that fit every part of his army career, suggesting a rough sequence.

First, induction, or encounters with an alien way of life; then learning technical skills and enduring the rigorous training, both of which mature him; then a focus on the skills the army chooses to use, practiced in the semitropical jungles and swamps of Florida. Throw in some attention to the general life-in-the-military experiences such as payday, passes, train rides and, finally, the not entirely smooth transition back to civilian life.

Shepherd tells his army stories, indeed all his stories, in no special order—randomly it seems—each self-contained. Once one begins to cull them and organize them, however, they suggest a coming-of-age-in-the-army narrative that can reasonably be deemed Jean Shepherd's Army Life Novel.

THE REAL, AND UNREAL, SHEP

For many people, influenced by his intimate, first-person radio style, Shepherd's stories, spoken and written, appear intensely autobiographical, but—brace yourselves—they ain't. Even when he is consciously trying to remember his life, Shepherd has a hard time keeping a straight face. He has a penchant for mischievous deception, even outright obfuscation and self-contradiction, when describing the "facts" of his life to reporters. For those who know his works, his comments the year before he died tell it like it probably was: "I want my stuff to sound real. And so when I tell a story, I tell it in the first person, so it sounds like (by the way, that's the best way to tell a story, in the first person), that it sounds like it actually happened to me. Well, it didn't."

Yet his work continues to be described as *memoir*. As he several times commented over the years, memoir suggests mere remembering instead of creating, and *nostalgia* suggests the past was somehow better than the present. In fact, even his earliest stories in *Playboy* are described in the magazine as "memoir," and "nostalgia," undoubtedly to Shepherd's chagrin. After the first few, those misleading tags were dropped in favor of "humor."

If he still manages to convince us that these stories are true, congratulate him for his artful stratagems. He probably does remember some actual parts of the stories he tells. The problem is that in the main, we don't know which parts he remembers and which parts he fabricates. Compounding the issue, the more we hear and read Shepherd's fiction, the more we find instances where, seemingly just to confuse us, he mixes in parts of his real autobiography. So, we must pause before accusing him of fiction, as well as accusing him of memoir. The real "truth" is that only someone who knew exactly how it really was to be a kid or a soldier could tell such "true-to-life" stories.

Some of his best known stories about growing up, including those amalgamated into the holiday-favorite film *A Christmas Story*, reveal a deeper, darker, less amusing undercurrent to his humor and incorporate a criticism of militaristic thought and behavior—in both military and civilian life. Shepherd referred to "Duel in the Snow or Red Ryder Nails the Cleveland Street Kid," the base story of the beloved film, as an antiwar tale. The film depicts how little Ralphie dreams of shooting the bad guys. He schemes to get a Red Ryder BB gun for Christmas, over adult protests that "you'll shoot your eye out." Ralphie, prized rifle in hand, is a personification of "armed and dangerous." The original tale, and its conversion into the film, can be seen as a parable about a nation's yearnings for increasingly lethal weaponry.

In one army tale he comments, "This story, like all good stories, has deeper implications, ramifications—and reverberations. Which are the worst. The reverberations get you later—as you bounce off the cushions, heading toward the side pocket, all of a sudden you get hit by the waves." The reverberations sometimes reveal dark elements. His army stories, though highly entertaining, are occasionally quite grim, even though they rarely deal directly with death. Even more than his kid stories, the army stories, like the following one, are parables.

> You know what's interesting—whenever I tell an army story that really deals with the war, people get very bothered and write angry letters—and yet they want me to tell army stories. Like the time I told the army story of riding back in the train. Riding back in the train sleeping on the coffin of a dead Pfc. This bothered a lot of people. And why? Well—war is war, you know? And really, it is what Sherman said it was.

General William Tecumseh Sherman, who himself set fire to the South, famously declared, "War is hell." Shepherd, whose army stories do not deal directly with bloody battlefields, only occasionally comments on the horrors of battle. As a humorist, he walks a line between the grimness of the fight and the despair of the man enlisted in perpetual bogus exercises and meaningless disciplines. He usually keeps this reality at a distance. Still, he finds ways to insert phantoms of this brutal reality. His "Company K," for instance, is almost certainly a literary homage to William March's *Company K*, an eyes-wide-open 1933 semi-autobiographical novel about World War I marines.

We might think about another connection as well. *Company K* deals with the brutality and horror of war. Although of a different order, the considerable discomforts endured by Shepherd's "Company K" incorporate his home–front-style version of a much more tolerable rung of hell. March's participants, in the thick of battle, still represent but a minority of those in uniform. Most conscripted souls remain far behind the front lines in much more comfortable circumstances. Shepherd knows that his rear-echelon, weary, overworked, underappreciated, demeaned, frustrated, and disgruntled enlisted men are the lucky ones despite their never-ending litany of complaints.

Shepherd's gripes are symptomatic of military lower echelons and are to be taken with a grain of Shep—he follows in the honorable tradition of military gripes, humorous, if often grimly so as found in Bill Mauldin's cartoons and in the popular comic strips *Beetle Bailey* and *Sad Sack.* Enlisted men are born to gripe.

ABOUT THE STORIES

Any attempt to connect the dots between stories will reveal a few bare patches. For example, Shepherd remains in Company K from the earliest tales of training in Camp Crowder through the later radar stories in Camp Murphy. An exception is his story of his radar studies, which don't mention Company K and its relocation to Florida. And don't be concerned if Lieutenant Cherry is sometimes promoted to Captain Cherry. He's the company commander, and his rank is of little importance—except to him.

These stories form a mostly unflattering but inevitably amusing portrait of his military world. Some of the humor is low key, while some of it is based on unexpectedly outrageous exaggeration. Only a few of his army stories describe the sometimes cruel military mind, but lest we think that he holds himself separate from such depictions, he at times implicates not only his fellow soldiers but himself as well in inhumane behavior. Examples include a version of the pole-climbing experience in which the corporal in charge has an acrophobic private hoisted fifty feet up a pole, where he is left dangling in the wind and dark, crying and screaming for hours. That chilling story is included here, with another pole-climbing incident—a nearly fatal tale, but ending on a comic note. Another story, sometimes titled "Shermy the Wormy," follows a nerdy misfit who is teased and sadistically tormented by Shepherd and his buddies. These kinds of stories, not often found in Shepherd, represent the dark side of the human character that the stresses and constrictions of military life can expose.

Shepherd often presents a hilariously unflattering view of humanity and of the military as a grotesque fraternity, but one should never conclude that he is even remotely unpatriotic. His negative comments are those of a disappointed lover who wants America to measure up to its own ideals. Pay attention to the deep undercurrent of patriotism he exhibits in "Fourth of July in the Army."

Throughout his story-telling career, Shepherd tended to deride fictional descriptions of life as incomplete or overly dramatic. As he did in one army episode about a forced march:

> You continually see stories and movies and plays about the army, but I can tell you, I have never seen anything that even remotely resembles the real army. It's always the way a writer sees the army, or it's the way a writer who was in the army wished that the army was when he was in it. You know, like dramatic. It never is. So he writes it when he gets out. Where you get the fascistic

second lieutenant, and the little corporal who's a young Jewish boy from Brooklyn who's gonna get killed, who says beautiful things and writes poems, and he's gonna have a little grocery store on Flatbush Avenue when he gets back. And you know he's gonna get killed. And this new lieutenant played by Van Johnson comes in and they all hate him from the beginning. I never saw any of that in the army.

He revels in observing and reporting otherwise infrequently noted "everyday life as it really is," whether he finds it in a mess line or waiting in line at the dry cleaners at 85th and Broadway. The KP skimped on his serving of SOS. The cleaner failed to remove a spot on a customer's trousers but removed a five-spot from his pocket. So many of these minor incidents pass by us nearly unnoticed.

THE KIDS VS. THE GIS

Shepherd's kid stories and his army stories are the most popular part of his creative career. For those who also consider his kid stories to be the best part of his work, here is his comment from a broadcast late in his radio career: "And by the way, for those of you who think kid stories made me what I am today [laughs], you're crazy. Not at all. They've held me back from what I should have been." You see, stories—especially kid stories—are but an element of what he accomplished on the air. He seems dismayed that he is most celebrated for his stories about being a child. Yes, the kid stories are highly entertaining, perceptive, and funny, but maybe Shepherd's kids—with their stories—should be taken down a peg.

His overall work in radio includes so much non-story material, ingredients that in their totality incorporated so much originality, that story-telling is just one strong component of his accomplishment. And here is the kicker: many of his kid stories, as good as they are, remain more of a surface affair, while his army stories, especially those in this book, often rise to a more serious—albeit humorous—level, depicting soldiers forced to put away childish things and encounter adult life with its adversities that sometimes morph into difficult epiphanies. They constitute the army-inspired *bildungsroman* that made Jean Shepherd a man.

—*Eugene B. Bergmann*
April 2013

PART ONE

YOU'RE IN THE ARMY NOW!

*J*ean Shepherd told various stories about his first encounters with army life. (He indicated several times that he was seventeen at the time, but official army records indicate that he joined in 1942 at age twenty.) What was it like to face this unfamiliar situation as a young man? These were his first eye-opening days of learning—not the Signal Corps subjects he was there for—but the overriding lessons of what it was like to be in an enormous institution with its inexplicable ways of acting in the world. He also learned something more about what life in general was like:

> That's one of the great things about being in the armed forces. You learn a lot more about stuff than you ever do in real life—in fact that's real life! The lives that most of us lead are kind of make-believe lives in our world. But in the army it comes right out. There it is. It comes right out. You see, people tend to think that the world that we live in, our daily world—that this is the real world and the army is a kind of artificial situation, when actually, according to Shepherd's famous "one-hundred-eighty-degree phase-shift-theory-of-truth syndrome," it's exactly the opposite! The truth comes out in the army, and the truth is very muted in our own daily lives.

Shepherd felt disappointed by his induction into this alien world. As his world was about to change, the system didn't even attempt to promote in him the sense of importance he expected to feel. In one *early encounter, naïve as he was, he even tried to be funny—and he got away with it. Near the beginning of the war and Shepherd's part in it, while the military was still gearing up to its full potential, the large influx of inductees, recruits were "orientated" into the world of war—not quite the Hollywood version they had grown up with at the picture show. Shepherd began to train his ear to GI-talk and learn how to speak the lingo.*

These first disorienting days of army life were spent, according to Shepherd, at Fort Sheridan, Illinois, a major recruit reception center north of Chicago. After this short orientation, he and his new buddies would be transported to the glories of early Signal Corps schooling in the Ozarks.

—EB

INDUCTION

War. Okay, you got the scenery? War brings up a lot of images when I say the word. I'll say it again: WAR. Some of the images are good, too. Like heroism. Men with a mission. We are climbing the hills to protect the world for democracy or whatever it might be. Then, of course, there's the other side. The other side you don't even know about. But it's the in-between side where you really learn things. Because you never learn anything from the actual scenes of violence you see in war. For one thing they're too quick, too fast, too loud, and too many other things are happening for you to actually learn anything from them. Do you learn anything from an automobile accident on the turnpike? You don't. You think you do but you don't.

So it's the in-between things, not the violent ones, okay? So I'm seventeen years old and not really shaving yet. I have seen Don Ameche movies, I have seen Errol Flynn giving it to the enemy in the Pacific. You know all the old movies you see on TV? You're scared to go and at the same time there's a mission. It's a very complicated feeling at the time it's actually going on.

Before I realized it, I filled out some forms in a rash moment in high school. They told me if I filled them out it would be okay, I wouldn't have to go for a long time and they'd send me to school. All they wanted was my name on the line and they got it. It took me about ten minutes to get home and the orders were already there in a big fat envelope that told me where I had to go. Immediately I feel very heroic and people have parties for me, congratulating me. I'm all excited and hollering and I drink a glass of beer and everything and eventually the day comes.

I was thinking all these images—I'm going to get *examined*, and they were going to swear me in. Well, when you hear the phrase "swearing in," have you ever seen this done in the movies? It's very dramatic, isn't it? So I arrived at Franklyn Street in downtown Chicago. Right in the middle of the Loop. It's an office building. There is a slight mist coming down. It's raining. I am prepared for something official, an event like a graduation. I am going to become changed; it is historical.

"Okay, you guys, you're in the army. All right, you're in the army." We've just been sworn in. You know that wonderful swearing in where Van Johnson talks and the guys cry? The thing where they play "The Star Spangled Banner"? It's all over. We didn't hear anything! And one of the guys calls out, "What about the oath?" And the corporal says, "You just heard it. Get the potatoes out of your ears, mac!" We didn't hear anything! We wanted something to happen, you know? Where is it? When does the balloon go up? And we stand around and the corporal yells, "Get out! There's another bunch comin' in!" And they push us toward the door and there's the other bunch coming in, so a couple of us holler, "Hey, they're going to give you the oath! Hey, fellows, it's the oath!" And a couple of these guys, you could see their eyes brighten a little bit and then the captain and the corporal start mumbling again.

Gradually we go down, out onto the street, and it's still raining, and it's all over. All over. I'm now in the army. I'm one with Errol Flynn and Don Ameche and all those guys who broke through the Western Front in the movies.

SHORN

I remember the day. I got this letter, see. It wasn't a draft letter. I wasn't drafted actually, I was in the enlisted reserve. I joined the enlisted reserve right in high school. The whole point of staying in the enlisted reserve corps is that you were supposed to be out of the army for a while. So here comes this letter. It said, the following EM will report for active duty. That was the first time I was ever called EM. I didn't even know what it meant.

So I was going to Fort Sheridan, which is a big induction center outside of Chicago. I got off the train and fell in with the crowd. Around the end of the platform came two big army trucks. A guy got out and walked across the platform. I noticed he had two big stripes on his sleeve. He said, "All right, you guys. How many of you guys are reportin' today for induction at Fort Sheridan, heh?"

Everybody's hand went up.

"All right, you guys, divide up in two groups. You guys fill up the first truck, guys left over get in the second truck, come on, on the double. Let's move."

We ran like mad across the platform and into the trucks. Nobody said anything. Everybody was kind of unfriendly yet because we were still civilians. One of the key characteristics of the civilian life is that hardly anybody feels any connection with anybody else. You don't walk down the street in New York and see a bunch of guys wearing coats and suits and say, "Ah, a fellow-civilian. Put 'er there, buddy." We got down to the post gate, about a ten-minute ride, and right through the gate we went.

We were all peering around. We saw all these buildings. I had my little bag and I had my Dopp kit that my Aunt Glen gave me for a going away present. I had the three dollars I'd saved in my money belt around my waist. All GIs get a money belt. That's the first thing they get and the first thing they throw away. We stopped in front of a big building and the same guy with the two stripes walked out around and said, "All right, you guys, fall out, fall out, let's go, on the double, move, let's move it there, shake it up."

Remember we were enlisted reserves. We were already in the army, you follow me? We'd already been through our physicals, so we didn't have to get it again and maybe get rejected. We were in. Ain't gonna be no escape for this crowd.

He lined us all up and there we stood. Little did we realize that in the next thirty minutes, a nasty, dirty, stinking trick was about to be perpetrated on us that would forever change our attitude both toward ourselves and our environment.

He looked up and down the line and he asked each guy's name and checked each guy off on his clipboard. "Straighten up, pull in your gut." First time anyone's told the guy to pull in his gut. Your mother doesn't call it your gut. "All right, all you guys, atten-hut! That means attention. Pull in your gut. Left face. I said left face, you stupe. Left face. Forward harch! Hut hup hip hup. Hut hup hip hup. Hut hup hip hup."

We were clumping along. You felt very foolish the first time you did that. You ever think how foolish the first time you walk with a whole bunch of strangers—in step? And there was a guy running along beside you going "Hut hup hip hup." You felt like some kind of idiot. We were walking along, going up and down with our feet. They don't tell you where you're going. We were just going, see. Hut hup hip hup. Hut hup hip hup. We were going along the big, long, muddy street. Hut hup hip hup between all the white buildings, and once in a while you saw the skulking eyes of another victim peering out of the windows at you. "Hut hup hip hup. Hut hup hip hup. Hut hup hip hup one two three *halt*! At ease, you guys, and that means don't talk. Shut up, don't talk, just stand at ease. Wait till further orders."

We stood. In front of a white building. Where it is about to happen. Strange ritual—which is oddly—and totally—humiliating. Because man is a creature of ego. Man is one of the few creatures who thinks about his appearance. It is not yet recorded that a racing horse knows it's beautiful. Does your dog think he's cute? Do you ever find your dog looking in the mirror saying, "Oh, what a cute bunch of—look at that! Am I lucky I'm a dachshund! Look at them ears—oh, aren't they cute!"

Oh no. It is only man who constantly and eternally peers into mirrors admiring himself. Adorning himself, thinking endlessly about how to make himself look cuter. So how do you strike at man? How best would you like to reduce him to rubble? That's right. Strike where it counts!

A sergeant pops out of this white building—and this was the first time we had seen a sergeant—and he had stripes that ran from his shoulder right down to his elbow. A gnarled, grizzled type. "All right, you guys, get in a column of threes. When I call out, each three of ya, I want all you first three guys to come in when I call out for the first three. I want the second three to come in when I call out for the second three. I don't want any of youse guys talkin' out here, I don't want ya runnin' away, you stay right here. This won't take long. I don't want any messin' around 'cause we gotta get this over wit. All right, you guys, first three, let's go."

The first three trotted in after him. A little scared. I was in the second group, one of the few times I've almost been at the beginning of a line. I was standing in the first three now. We didn't know what was going to happen. The first group hadn't been gone for forty-five seconds when the sergeant stuck his head out and said, "All right, next three, come on, let's go, on the double, let's move it."

The three of us ran like hell because we didn't want to get into trouble, see. One guy was a big, fat guy from Rushmore, Indiana, and the guy behind me was a tall, skinny guy from Peoria. We ran like mad into the place.

I couldn't believe it! I thought they were going to give us uniforms or something. But this strange place. A long hall. And there must have been seventy-five barber chairs and there were no mirrors! No mirrors at all! And there was a Pfc standing behind each barber chair. The first three guys were putting on their jackets, looking very strange. Like three turnips were putting on coats. I never saw such a sight in my life. Their eyes were staring and wild.

I sat down in the first chair that the Pfc pointed at. The other two guys sat down. The Pfc put a white thing around me, which was familiar. All men are familiar with that white thing. Then came the strange feeling. The next thing that happened was totally unfamiliar. Suddenly around my whole head there was a cloud, a nimbus. It was like raining hair *zzzaaaaaaaaaaaaaaaaaaaaaaawaaaaa*.

Oh, my god! The pride of my life since I was twelve, and the one thing that I owned that was mine, that was my most beautiful possession—my magnificent D. A. I had one of the most beautiful D. A. haircuts you ever saw in your life. And I would comb it. It was gigantic, it was huge, a big thing in the front and I would comb it in the back where it came together and it would stick out and would feather out over the ears. Oh, it was beautiful. Tremendous. And I used to put stuff in it and fix it all up when I had a date with Esther Jane. I would comb it and brush it and I would look in the mirror at it and look at the side view at it. I'd say, "Oh, what a fantastic creature you are." And I would fluff it up again, and more I would comb it.

And now this guy—he's got ahold of my left ear and he's holding it like you hold a jackhammer. And he was twisting it, and he had in his right hand this machine, and he was starting up over my right ear and he was going *waaaaaaaaaaaa aaaaawawawaaaaa*. It stuck in the back where it was thickest and most beautiful *aaaaawawawaaaaa aaaaawawawaaaaa*. And I felt this breath of cold air suddenly, this tremendous cold all around me! I couldn't believe it! It was like I was in a refrigerator!

And it was off. All over. "All right, mac, let's go, next one, let's go, let's move it on, let's move it outta here, you guys." And then the final insult. The Pfc behind the chair says, "Seventy-five cents, mac." Uh! You gotta pay for this! I reached in my pocket. Seventy-five cents! I had a buck in my pocket my uncle Tom gave me when I got on the bus. I gave the guy the buck and he gave me a quarter back.

Then it began to slowly seep into me. I probably looked worse than I'd ever looked in my life. I felt the back of my neck. It was strange. Strange. My skin had turned to sandpaper. There was a thick, hard, angry stubble all the way up the back, and I could feel that the bottom of my neck was turning red from the clippers and the machines. My ears—amazing—my ears had suddenly slipped down. I had ears way down on the bottom of my head. My head stuck up like a big radio tube, it was like a bulb on the top. And the guy ahead of me from Rushmore, Indiana, the big fat slob who had had this long, black hair, which was obviously the pride of his life, now looked like a human pyramid. He looked fantastically bad. Nothing looks worse than a guy with jet black hair who's had a close, a really close army haircut. I saw a big scar on top of his head that had healed over, like when he was two and he fell out of bed or something. The guy behind me from Peoria was crying. Out in the sunlight we saw seven or eight guys from our little company who had already had the thing done. We went back to our place in line and the wind was blowing *whooooooo hooooooooooooooo,* and it was cold. You felt the cold air hitting the top of your ears.

Within ten minutes I had totally ceased to be a civilian. I was something else now. And all those other guys around me were something else, too. It was then that I heard my first true, heartfelt, army gripe. Up to that point we didn't gripe, we just sort of went along. The guy next to me said a word. Well, somehow it sounded right. Just sounded right. You could see little flecks of his hair all over the back of his coat.

The sergeant stood out in front of us with the corporal and he looked at us, about forty-five of us. He walked up and down, his overseas hat pulled down low over his brow, sharp as a tack, the kind of guy who wore tailored fatigues. "All right, you guys, you look a lot betta. Got rid of all that excess junk hangin' on ya. Now we're gonna really start straightenin' ya up. Ten-hut! You're gonna hear that a lot in the next few years. When I say ten-hut, that means you just don't move, you pull in your gut, you put your feet right where they should be, heels together, toes out at the proper, prescribed angle. Left face. Forward harch!

We marched into the middle distance. We marched into the middle distance with the breeze blowing around our ears. With the wind blowing over the top of what little fuzz of our former civilian ego was left. We marched into the middle distance. Changed. Converted. A new breed. We were soldiers. Oh, yes.

Hair is important. It could change your whole life. Hut hup hip hup. Hut hup hip hup. Hut hup hip hup. No mirrors. You gotta strike where it's most vulnerable—the ego. The ego.

D IS FOR DRUID

I'm accepted, I've gone through my physical and everything else and I have been sworn in. I can't back out. I'm in the army and we're going through another long line and there are guys writing down information on you. And here's a tech sergeant sitting there with five stripes, looking very official. He looks up from his forms and he says to me, "Your religion, please. Give me your religion."

I say, "I...I... don't have any religion."

"What do you mean you don't have any? What religion are you? A Jew?"

I say, "No, no."

"Ya Catholic?"

"No."

"Okay, you're Protestant."

"No!" It's always assumed by a lot of people that if you're not Jewish, if you're not Catholic, you're a Protestant. Now, wait a minute. That's making a hell of an assumption! Pardon that I use a religious term. After all, Hell is a religious concept.

And he says, "You're a Protestant."

I say, "No, I'm not. What do you mean? I'm not a Protestant." And I'm holding up the line. There are a lot of guys behind me. I say, "What has that got to do with anything? Really, I don't have any religion."

He says, "What are you, an atheist?"

"What's an atheist?"

"It's a guy who don't believe in any of them religions."

"Well, I can't say that! I can't say I'm an atheist, really, just because I can't say what I believe. I just don't have any religion."

"Well," he says, "ya gotta put something on your dog tags! Something on my dog tags!

He says, "Do you know there's a regulation that on your dog tags there has to be stamped your name, your serial number, your blood type, and your religion."

This is a new concept to me so I decide I'm going to be funny. All my life I've gotten into trouble like this. Some people have no sense of humor at all, and I've discovered that you can get yourself into one hell of a mess by just being funny about what most people don't see anything funny in! So I say, "I'll tell you what, put me down as a Druid."

He puts his pen down, looks up, and he says, "You're a what?!"

"A Druid. Put me down as a Druid. A Druid. It doesn't matter one way or the other. Put a D down on my dog tags for Druid."

He says, "We don't have no D. We either have C for Catholic, J for Jew, you have P for Protestant, or A for Atheist. We don't have no D. Now what is a Druid?"

I say, "Druidism is a religion. We believe in oak trees and stuff and we have a scroll, see. What we do, we believe in the great god of the forest."

"What do you mean, the great god? Do you go to church?"

"Oh, yes, well, not really. Our church is the forest and we go out on a Sunday and we sit under the oak trees and we read from a birch bark scroll about the great god of the forest."

He calls out, "Hey, lieutenant!" I'm standing there and I think I'm being funny, but at this point it's beginning to escalate. They don't realize that at that point I'm only seventeen and I really don't know a lot about the bureaucracy, and when he turns and hollers for the lieutenant, I should have said, "Oh, put anything down." At that point the lieutenant walks over and says, "Yes, sergeant?"

Sergeant says, "This man here says he's a Druid. I ask him what his religion is, he says he's a Druid."

The lieutenant says, "Is this true?" By the way, the lieutenant obviously knows what a Druid is. He says, "You *are* a Druid?"

At this point I am deeply committed. Guys all around me, waiting in line. "Yes," I say. "Yes, sir."

He says, "Well, put down a D for him, sergeant."

The sergeant says, "A D, sir. We only have Catholics, Protestants, Jews, and Atheists, but I haven't put down a D yet, sir."

He says, "Write a D down for him."

The sergeant writes D down in the place where it says religion.

I don't think anything about it until about a week later, after they have issued my dog tags. I don't even know what all the numbers are. There's a little D on the bottom of my dog tags. So one day, after I've been in my first army company for about two weeks, we come back from a hike and the first sergeant is out there with his clipboard, about to let us go back to the barracks and he says, "Will the following men report to the orderly room," and he reads a bunch of names. Then he reads my name. "Is Private Shepherd here?"

I say "Yes, sir."

"Will you report to the chaplain."

"Report to the chaplain?"

"Yeah, report to the chaplain as soon as you can. He definitely wants to talk to you. In fact you can do it before chow."

Well, we're going to have chow in about twelve minutes. So I walk to the chaplain's office. I don't know what this is about. Who knows? I'm going to get a leave or something. Any time anyone goes to the chaplain in our company it's because his grandmother got hit by a truck and they're going to break it to him gently, or the guy applied to OCS and got in, or something like that.

So I walk in and the chaplain is sitting there, rimless glasses, he's got a little cross on the collar, and he's a captain. He says, "Sit down, soldier."

"Yes, sir."

"I have your Form 32 here. It says that you're a ... under religion it says D. Explain that to me."

It happened what seems like years before and fifty-thousand things happened to me between then and now. "D? Oh, yes, sir. I'm a Druid"

"You're a Druid? I'm curious. What church do you attend?"

"Well, we Druids don't attend church, sir."

He says, "You know, I've studied you in theology. I'd really like to talk to you about your religion." He is fascinated! "Druidism is a very interesting religion," he says.

I say, "Yes, sir." I do not know a damn thing about Druidism!

He says, "I'd like to spend some time discussing it with you."

I say, "Yes, sir."

Two days later I'm transferred. I might add, I'm probably the only registered Druid in the history of the contemporary army.

BEING ORIENTATED

For a while I was in a real fighting outfit, and I'll never forget learning about war. This was when I first got in the army and I was a kid. I'd grown up on Errol Flynn and Van Johnson, and I had ideas—I knew who the good guys were—and the bad guys. And I was always looking for that lieutenant who looked like Van Johnson, who was gonna lead me up to the pillbox, take that difficult hill, and all that. And I kept looking around for the guy who was going to be killed—you know—the tall, lanky kid from Brooklyn, whose father had the grocery store and he had just gotten married and he got a letter saying his wife had just had a baby? And in all the stories, he jumps around and hollers? And says, "Woopie! Hot diggety dog!" And shows everybody the picture and you know he's going to get killed in the next reel? I never met that guy in the army, actually. I know a guy who also got a letter about having a baby, but all he did was turn green. Of course, that's another story.

Anyway, they take us down to this corrugated iron hut where they showed movies in this camp. It had a lot of sawdust on the floor and wooden seats and all that—this was the beginning of the war, you know.

In all the Hollywood movies that I'd ever seen about the war, we were winning. I mean, seriously. Any kind of movie—even the newsreel movies—we were winning. I'd just seen things like, *Give Them the Business in Burma*, when Don Ameche and Errol Flynn would drop behind the lines—oh, terrible things happened to the Japs immediately. Well, I'd been brought up on that, and this was the first movie I ever saw like this one. I'll never forget it. I'm sitting there on my little wooden seat, wearing my big tin hat, and I'm surrounded by all of these near-sighted guys who had come into the army with me—skinny, roughly seventeen years old, transparent, skin troubles, all of us who were just out of the *Little Orphan Annie* stage and just about to begin reading *Spicy Western* when the army got us.

We were sitting there. An officer came out and said, "Men, you are about to be orientated. I am the orientation officer in this organization and I'll tell you this, I can orientate a dog! There hasn't been a man yet come through this command who hasn't left here thoroughly orientated. Now a lot of you guys don't know what orientation means. Well, after today's session, you are going to have a slight idea of what it means to be orientated by First Lieutenant Jack Gurney. I am the best orientation officer in the entire Second Army. Any of you guys want to argue about it? I'll be willing to take on any of you guys—I'll take off these bars and man-to-man I'll orientate ya. All right, corporal, will you please turn on the machine."

The lights went down and on came the movie. It showed a bunch of German soldiers, square-jawed, silver eyes, swimming a river like machines—in formation. And a voice said, "You are now seeing a film of a German bangalore torpedo team going into action against a pillbox on the Maginot Line. Watch carefully, men. This is a magnificently performed, a magnificently executed maneuver."

We were watching and it was gray and all fuzzy and you see the tracers coming out of the pillbox *dacadacadaca-dacadacadacadacadacadacadaca*. These German films—I don't know where they got *cadacadacadacadaca*. I was looking for Errol

Flynn. I was looking around for Van Johnson, *dacadacadacadaca, shuush shuush shush,* once in a while a rocket shuush shuush shush, and I saw these guys swimming across the river and these guys were carrying with them something on their back—I never saw anything like it. Suddenly they deployed on the opposite bank. You should have seen it. It was fantastic. These guys fanned out and they looked nothing like any of the guys I was in the army with. With that, one by one they began to crawl forward *dacadacadacadac.* Suddenly they leaped up, six of them, with a bangalore torpedo, up they went dacadacadacadac, right up to the side of the pillbox *boooooommmmm!* No pillbox. No soldiers in it. All of them gone. Fantastic! Bangalore torpedo maneuver.

And with that, the next voice said, "Now you are about to watch a strafing raid on the streets of Rotterdam photographed through the gun cameras of a Stuka. You will have to excuse the shaky condition of the film because these were taken in action." Dacadacadacadaca. These guys were hitting everybody. They didn't miss anything, Dacadacadacadacadacadacadacadaca, This guy was going along pickling off street lights as he dove down! *Dacadacadacadaca, booooooooommm! Dacadacadacadaca,* some clown went down the street on a bicycle—this guy shot out his tires first! Then knocked his toolkit off and then pow! between the eyes! *Dacadacadacadaca,* All the while I was watching for Van Johnson. The lights came up.

I was sitting there with my wooden gun—they had given me a wooden gun the day before, carved cleverly to resemble a British Enfield, which went out of action forty-eight years before in the last skirmish of the Boer War.

I was sitting there. The first lieutenant came out and said, "You are now on your way to being orientated." Little did he realize how much he was speaking the truth.

ARMY PHRASEOLOGY

I spent a few years in the company of many other guys wearing the same suits, so I was fascinated when a guy said recently, "Can you imagine what would happen if somebody decided to really *do* a play or a novel, or a movie, where they actually used real GI language?" What a fantastically funny movie it would be! I had to laugh like hell, because it's quite true that the civilian believes that GI language consists of one word. Oh no! GI obscenity is extremely rich and varied. And all the expressions have a basic underlying humor. The subject of GI humor, the genuine thing, has rarely been explored by an ex-GI. Mostly it's been written about by a professor who was never near the scene.

I can think of a number of great expressions that the civilian has never heard in his life. "Give us a sample," you say? Are you kidding? Stuff that's pretty innocent, for example, has a name in the army, which, if I used, would get me banned for life from all media. I can't give any of it here.

You've been down to the deli and bought cold cuts, so the army has a term for cold cuts. In addition, there are terms that differentiate *between* cold cuts. If you get liverwurst you get one term, and if you get baloney you get another. Innocent potatoes have a name that would get me banned. GI expressions are fantastic. For another example, they have a great expression for beds.

If you were in the air force or navy or the marines or something, you'd have a whole series of different phrases with some crisscrossing where the phraseology would be the same. And these are not "old fashioned terms," these are still used in various army elements around the world, and yet they don't have much to do with the kind of language that is used in novels about the army.

I'll never forget my first five minutes in the army. I couldn't believe it. Here I was from the steel mills. You cannot grow up in a steel mill town and live a sheltered existence at the same time. Every conceivable kind of language had flowed into one ear and out the other, and I'd played three years of high school football. I'd heard a lot of stuff. But five minutes after I was in the army, a guy opened a door and hollered something—I flipped! I laughed for about twenty minutes. I said, "The army's gonna be really wild if they talk like this!"

What kind of stuff am I talking about? Well, first of all, the army, of course, has innumerable variations on various bodily functions. But that's the obvious. It also has names for almost everything that you have in your ordinary life, a name which had at one and the same time an erotic/obscene/funny connotation. Even a little, innocent thing. So a guy's sitting in the mess hall with coffee in front of him and he wants to put some cream in it. He looks down the table and he sees they've got the pitcher with cream. What does he call it? Does he say, "Ah, would you please pass the cream?" Are you kidding?!

I remember the third day I'm in the army and I'm standing in line in the mess hall. The word is immediately passed back all down the line as to what they are having today. So I'm standing there, a brand new private, and the guy in front of me says, "Hey, oh, damn it!" with a blast of obscenity.

I say, "What's the matter?"

He says, "Ah, I forgot it's Wednesday. I wouldn't even have come to this damn mess hall today."

"What's the matter?"

"I'll go to the PX and get myself some Milky Ways."

"Why?"

And then he tells me what they had, and I had no idea what he meant! It wasn't SOS, which is what civilians think they're always saying.

So I say, "What? What's that?"

The guy behind me says, "Oh no! Oh wow!" He heard it and passes it along, and immediately guys in the back of the line start to peel off. And I peel off, I trot away with them. I figure, well, I'm in the army, I'll learn how to do it. So I peel off with them and five minutes later we're all down at the PX eating Powerhouse candy bars washed down by lukewarm Coke. I didn't know what the stuff was, so a couple of days later I'm back in the line again and a guy tells another guy, and I'd heard the phrase before. I turn to the guy behind me and say, "They've got blahblahblah." And the guy says, "Oh damn," and he turns. Some stay and some don't. There's a certain kind of guy in the army called a "chow hound," who, if they serve rocks, would stay. The idea of getting free food to him is so fantastic that he just wouldn't quit. If they gave him rocks with gravy he'd stay there and eat the gravy and the rocks. He'd come back for seconds.

So I stay in line. I get up to the front of the line and there it is! I discover what this stuff is that they were talking about. And I know why they'd peeled off. At which point it's too late because you don't peel off when you're up there at the food tray, because the minute you do that, the mess sergeant standing there says, "What are you doing! What do you want? You're in line here, buddy!" And so you go through the line. Well, that's one moment of revelation.

I must also add that various infirmities that accompany the human body through time and space have certain very colorful phrases which I am sure many members of the medical fraternity would enjoy knowing about, because they are very apt.

PART TWO

ARMY HOSPITALITY

From all evidence, the army packed Shepherd and his comrades off to an alien part of the country that went by the name of Camp Crowder, Missouri, near the town of Neosho. Sometimes the customs and requirements of his new environment were merely odd, sometimes dangerous, almost always obnoxious, yet, on occasion, surprisingly pleasant. Regarding things pleasant, in at least two stories, Shepherd pays tribute to the beauty of the local hillbilly girls, exemplified by Daisy Mae, the pulchritudinous young thing right out of Al Capp's popular comic strip, Li'l Abner.

Shepherd touches on what he calls "folk art," his encounter with an army piano virtuoso. An emotional and patriotic episode, "The Fourth of July in the Army," shows Shepherd's strong love of America. As originally broadcast, it is a good example of his fantastic audio skills—he adds sound effects solely with his own voice and skillfully uses music, particularly "Stars and Stripes Forever."

The twenty-four-hour-a-day infirmities at Camp Crowder conclude with a train ride from hell. Though he endures that journey with a serious, mysterious illness, his escape from Camp Crowder culminates in what Shepherd describes as "a miracle cure." He is well again, delivered from hell to what seems like paradise, as he and his comrades *disembark in the warmth of the semitropical deep South. There they will spend most of their military service in a secret Signal Corps radar unit—encountering heat, humidity, and other torments in and around Florida's famous and glorious swamp—another form of hell.*

—EB

SHERMY THE WORMY

Down at the end of the barracks was a guy who had ridden in the troop train with us all the way from Fort Sheridan. He was a little round guy. He was older than we were. We were about seventeen to nineteen. This guy was probably twenty-five or so. He was of indeterminate age. Little round man who parted his hair in the middle, and he had what we used to call in Hessville, Indiana, a cookie duster—a little moustache—and it was one of those *snooty* little moustaches. He was the kind of guy who was always making those little niggling comments, complaints like, "When are they going to do something about *this*?" He had the soul of an insurance man. This little guy sitting there. And yet, on the other hand, he was very harmless. He never did anything, never argued, always did his stuff. But he was *different*. He had a moustache. That was the only difference I could see except that he was sitting there in a different sort of way from the rest of us. Men have a way of sitting that says, "I'm *here*! I'm *really* here and I'm part of the scene," and the rest of us were sitting that way, but he wasn't.

The whistle blew and everyone got up and went outside. We stood in a long line in the company street. The duty sergeant walked back and forth, and he said, "Now look, you're here to learn how to be a soldier. This is the toughest outfit in the whole Signal Corps. You guys are *combat* signal men. You know what that means? You gonna find out!" We were saying to ourselves, "Yeah." And yet all the while there was a certain nice, lithe, animal quality of seventeen- and eighteen-year-olders, who have made the scene, who have a '41 Ford back home, the chicks, the whole thing. We were standing there. We weren't scared. We'd seen enough movies, we knew who was going to win this war. Don't give us that jazz. Only the *bad* guys got killed. We knew we weren't bad guys. No problem there.

So we were all standing there and he was walking up and down, and he said, "Now we're going to have a GI party. In two minutes I want you to be out here in this company street dressed in your fatigues, and we're gonna go down to the supply room, we're gonna draw mops and buckets, and we are gonna clean every inch of that barracks. Captain Cherry is gonna be in tomorrow morning and he's gonna inspect this barracks with a toothbrush. We are gonna win the prize this week for the cleanest barracks. And if you don't win that plaque you ain't gonna go into Neosho next week." Neosho, Missouri, the town near the camp. Neosho had five hundred hillbillies, all suffering from hookworm. Nothing you wanted more than to go into Neosho.

But sure enough, we went tearing into the barracks. There was something about man hurling himself into an unpleasant task! You have to see it to understand it—*boom*! we go, guys on the floor rubbing and grubbing around, everybody sweating. I was on the top floor on my knees with twenty other guys scrubbing down the barracks with the GI brushes and the GI soap. We were washing down everything.

And over at the other end of my line of brush-wielders was Sherman, more popularly known as Shermy the Wormy. Shermy, with his little snotty cookie duster, was down on his knees scrubbing like mad. He couldn't keep up with us seventeen-year-olds. We were going, "Come on, let's go, you idiot," and he was way back, and the poor little guy was huffing and puffing and sweating, and we finally arrived at the end, and all by himself, he was about a third of the way down.

And somebody said, "Come on, Shermy!"

And he said, "I'm hurrying."

"Come on, Shermy, let's go!"

We started cleaning the windows. That poor little guy was down there, scrubbing away. Three or four of us finished and we sat back. That great look of somebody who had done it. He'd cleaned his bit, he was through. "I ain't responsible." That spirit was okay when a guy was seventeen and he had that snotty, leaning-on-the-hood attitude. It was only dangerous when it persisted into adulthood. But there was a funny thing building up in the barracks. It was kind of an agreement—let's get after Shermy. Guys were saying things like, "Hey, Shermy, how about a cookie duster? You gonna shave it off for inspection, Shermy? Ha, ha!" Yeah, that kind of humor is great. Very subtle, see.

And Shermy was down there saying, "Oh, leave me alone, will you guys?"

Oh, what a mistake! What a mistake to say, "Leave me alone, guys."

"Hey, fellows, Shermy says to leave him alone."

Guys from downstairs became aware that something was going on and up they came, and Shermy was still on the floor trying to finish. And this duty sergeant starts up the stairs. Oh boy! You could hear him coming, *klump, klump, klump*! He stood there. All of us were standing around—we were done. And Shermy was on the floor. The sergeant hollered, "Get on the stick, you."

Shermy said, "Leave me alone, will you?"

The sergeant looked around and said with a smile, "Fellows, leave him alone." We had just gotten the okay from the authorities. He said, "Leave him alone, fellows."

Just like that, eighty-five guys went *boommm!* on Shermy. They all stood around Shermy: "Come on, Shermy." "You want me to help you, Shermy?" "Come on, I'll help you," and a guy grabbed his arm and they pushed the mop and they hit him. "Come on, get some more soap, will ya? Hey, get some soap."

And Shermy was still down there. And then Shermy started to cry—in the middle of the army! Some guy called out, "Hey Sergeant, what are we gonna do? Shermy's crying!" And we heard, way off down in the company street, "WHAT!"

We couldn't believe this. Somebody hollered out the window, "Hey, Sarge, Shermy's crying. Should we send him to the dayroom to rest?"

The Sergeant hollered, "Don't *bother* him, fellows." That was his way of saying, "Lay on, Macduff!" And Shermy was down there grubbling.

And it had to happen. One of the barracks wits started on the moustache. Apparently, all the years that poor little Shermy was an insignificant little guy, five feet four inches tall and five feet five inches wide, poor little Shermy's *only* thing of glory was that magnificent cookie duster. Which he had trimmed—beautiful little thing, like a little brush, and he was proud of it.

Somebody said, "Hey, Shermy, let me see your cookie duster, hee, hee. Hey, it tickles, fellows. Hey, Shermy, do the girls ever say anything when you kiss 'em? How does it feel kissing a girl when you have that moustache? Ha ha hoo hoo ha ha ha! Hey, fellows, come on, let's all line up and kiss Shermy!"

Sure enough, one lout was down on the floor saying, "Come on, Shermy, give me a kiss. I always wanted to kiss a girl with a moustache!"

And Shermy whimpers, "I'm not a girl." He was crying.

Well, it built up. It went like that until, finally, it had to come. Inevitably, you see, violence is like a cake of yeast. You add a little water, you set it out there in the sun, the sun shines down and it begins to rise. It rises higher and higher and higher until finally it reaches that moment when it is full-blown. Then somebody pricks it with a little pin and down it goes—it's completed the cycle. Somebody said, "Hey, Shermy, how'd you like to have me shave off your moustache?"

Shermy looked up. His face was white, just as white as a dishcloth, and he said, "You wouldn't do that!"

Boom! The guys knew what to do. Poor old Shermy had been touched on the sore tooth, and somebody said, "Come on, Shermy, let's go down to the latrine, Shermy. Let's shave off Shermy's moustache!" The guy yelled, "Hey, Sergeant, Sergeant, does the captain like guys with cookie dusters?"

Silence. That is the most sinister sound. That is the most sinister kind of approval. Silence. That's like calling for the cops, "Hey, cop, help me, hey, cop," and there's silence—he's looking the other way. The sergeant is just calmly walking down to the NCO club, and it's as though there on his back you can read SCHICK! It is there in big neon letters.

They all grab Shermy. *Boom!* Four thousand guys grab him. They have him by the feet and he's struggling, screaming and crying. And we go down the company street and GIs start pouring out of the other barracks. Thousands of them. "Hey, what are you doing, fellows?"

"We're shaving the cookie duster off Shermy! Shermy says it hurts to kiss a girl with a cookie duster. We're helping him out. We want to help Shermy get the girls in Neosho. Let's go."

And into the latrine we go, and ten guys hold him down and somebody whips out the shaving cream. I'm standing back and hollering like the rest, "Let's give it to him!" And his eyes! There are those two oysters looking up—those blue eyes looking at the ceiling. He's totally paralyzed. He's saying nothing now. And over him goes Gasser and does it—*keeech-keeech-keeech-keeech*. "Okay, Shermy, now you can go kiss a girl and she won't say it tickles."

Shermy gets up. Little flecks of shaving cream. Everybody standing around. Somebody says, "How does it feel, Shermy? Now you can feel the breeze again, can't you? Does it scratch? Does it itch?"

Shermy says nothing. Just turns around. Walks out of the latrine. The entire personnel of Company K stands there. Watches him go by. Somebody says, "Got any hot water? Boy, it's gonna be a great night in Neosho. Ah, boy, what a night. Let's go down and get our passes."

And we're all lined up getting our passes—except Shermy. Shermy is back in the barracks. Somewhere. Trying to grow a moustache. Trying to become six feet nine inches tall. Trying to lose forty pounds. Trying to become seventeen years old again. Trying to stop being this little round square who's scared of girls and scared of automobiles that honk, scared of dogs. He's down there in his upper bunk way down at the end with the covers pulled up.

And we're in Neosho. We all go into the Bamboo Inn. We sit down. There must be forty-five of us in this terrible, rotten clip joint. The kind of clip joint were it says, "Fifty girls, continuous show." And there's always a guy standing out front: "All right, let's go, let's go. The show is just beginning." We are in there, boy! Have you wondered who goes into those things? Sailors, soldiers. So we're sitting there drinking Rum Collins and stuff. And somebody hollers up at the emcee, "Hey, dedicate this next tune to Shermy," and the whole crowd breaks up.

This goes on for about fifteen minutes, when in comes a lieutenant. Never comes in this place. This is an enlisted man's joint. There are places that EMs go, and places that officers go, and it's an unwritten law—we have our territory, you have yours. And in comes this first lieutenant. He walks in and he's looking around. Everybody's sitting there wondering—what's he doing here? EM *here*, boy! There's a certain rugged pride in being the lowest thing on the face of the earth. You can't get any lower, they can't bust you, can't do nothin'!"

He walks through, "You guys from Company K?" This is in the middle of a nightclub! A singer is up there singing and a waiter's walking around with bottles of beer. "You guys from Company K?"

"Yeah, what do you want to make of it?" You know that attitude?

He says, "I'll tell you what I want to make of it. How many of you guys know Sherman?"

"Yeah, Shermy the girl!"

"You better get back to your company area, all of you." And he walks out. And you could feel it coming in from the street! There was a funny feeling. What happened? What happened? It just flowed in, and everyone thought, "What, is this guy putting us on?" That bravado! "Putting us on, ha, ha. He ain't gonna get *me* to go back, ha, ha!"

But everybody's saying, "It's kind of late, you know?" It is kind of late—we've been here eight minutes. I've had half a beer already! Kinda late! So we're all in that little red bus going back to Company K on Tennessee Avenue, the 27th Signal Corps Training Combat Battalion. We're all heading back. And, of course, everybody's talking about everything else but Shermy.

We get off the bus and there standing at the gate is a major in the MPs. Have you ever seen a major in the MPs? He's different from the little guy with the little white hat. A major is a *big* scene, you know!

Oh! And he's standing there by the gate where you present your pass. "All you guys from Company K? You guys from Company K, come over here. Come on, line up over here. I'm from the provost marshall. I want to know how many of you guys know Sherman." Every last one of us did. We want to know what happened. So somebody down at the end says, "We all know him, sir," still with a little bravado. "We all know him, sir, he's in our barracks."

"Sherman tried to hang himself tonight, and the first sergeant caught him in the barracks. I want to know which one of you was responsible. He won't talk. I just know somebody in this barracks did it."

And there we stand. Company K. Seventeen-year-old sharpies, all of us, our patches, our jazzy little hats with the Signal Corps braid. All standing there. Who caused it?

He says, "Listen, I want to find out who caused this and I want somebody to come down tomorrow morning to the provost marshall and give me a full story. Who is going to volunteer?"

And we stand. Nobody says a word. Ten minutes later we are in the barracks. And we can see, way down at the end, on the upper bunk, where they have rolled Shermy's bedding. It is rolled up and the blankets are gone and there is the GI ticking pillow.

He's gone out of our lives forever. But he's somewhere. And I suspect, right now, all over this country, there are at least a hundred and fifty guys out of Company K who—grown men wearing their Brooks Brothers suits and their jazzy Indian shirts—on quiet Saturday nights, walking through streets, occasionally see little round pasty faces with cookie dusters, with scared eyes, and they are reminded of something inside of them. Something inside each one of us. I can remember Shermy down on the floor saying, "Don't hurt me." And then those words, "Shermy says don't hurt him, fellows." Oh, yes, the army teaches you a lot of things.

GI GLASSES

Somehow or another they're going to give me an eye examination and decide if I need glasses. Glasses. All right, okay. Somehow the idea of getting a pair of glasses that you never had before is exciting. So I'm sitting in the clinic, about to get an eye exam. Incidentally, this is a place that later grew to rival in infamy Pearl Harbor itself. A place called Camp Crowder. Oh, it's incredible! And I'm sitting there in the Camp Crowder clinic. I'll never forget it. There are about forty-five guys around me, and all of these goof-offs are on sick call, but I'm here to get a pair of glasses.

Suddenly they wheel in a GI on a stretcher, and we look at him. He's watching us, and he says, "Hey fellows, will you call Company D and tell 'em I'm really sick. This is Olsen here."

I figure I'm going to do something about this guy, so I say, "Hey, doctor, this man is talking."

The doctor says, "Oh, don't worry about it, he's finished."

I say, "What?"

He says, "Yeah, he's got some rare disease. He's done. Don't worry about him. Next! Who's next?"

They give me an eye examination with a machine. With the little red crosses and yellow crosses. The technician says, "Tell me when you see the two lines come together. Tell me now when they cross." The crosses move. It's very official. A few minutes after I finish the exam a captain comes over to me and he says, "Okay, soldier, here's your glasses."

I put them on and they're really tight and they pinch my nose, and for the first time in my life, I can't see. I absolutely can't see! I walk around a bit and I say, "I can't see!"

"Ah, let's go, GI," the doctor says. "Next!"

I walk out into the sunlight and I take these things off and then I can see. As soon as I get back to my company area, the first sergeant calls me into the orderly room and says, "We've got a message from the clinic. You gotta wear your glasses all the time."

I say, "What do you mean? I can't see out of these things!"

"Wear the glasses!"

I walk out. The next day we're on the rifle range. I'm with my glasses. I can't see anything—there's three people moving around in front of me all the time. And they keep hollering, "Stand still, Shepherd, you're at attention!" This goes on for a week. I have a *splitting* headache! And every time I'm out with the company, the sergeant says, "Shepherd, you got your glasses on?" After that week, I finally go back to the clinic. I go in and see the captain and I say, "Captain, I can't see out of these glasses!"

He says, "Lemme see 'em. What's your name?"

"Shepherd, J. P., 11098946, sir."

He says, "No, you're not. You're Simonson, L. P., 350981642."

I say, "No, no!"

He looks at me for a bit. "I gave you the wrong glasses, soldier."

I say, "Oh! Now that solves the problem, sir. Please give me my glasses."

He gives me my glasses. They are dark green. I put them on and the world is black. For three-and-a-half years I carry these green glasses at the bottom of my army trunk. They cost the U.S. Army seventy-five dollars, I understand, and today I use them as a paper weight.

LIEUTENANT GEORGE L. CHERRY TAKES CHARGE

The guys were sitting around griping. Little did we realize how calm and how beautiful things were, until the day we faced a nervous moment. Company K is all lined up and our captain was standing out there in full dress, walking back and forth quietly in front of us.

"Men," he said, "I've got a special announcement. I didn't get to know a lot of you fellows the past months we've been together, but I have a special announcement to make that I think may be of some interest to all you men in Company K. Now I think you guys have got the makings of a good company. You ain't very good now, but you got the makin's."

We thought, what this going to be? What's up now? Because he had a certain solemn way about him and he was wearing his green dress jacket.

He said, "Men, today as of thirteen-hundred, this company is going to be in command of another officer." Whenever a big change comes into your life, there are two divergent thoughts, no matter what the change is. One: "Oh, no! No! Now what?" Then there's the other one: "Oh, wow! It's all gonna be better! Now things are really gonna be great!" You know, every organization I've ever worked in, there's the two opposing thoughts. So here was our company and we were being presented with this. For months now, we'd been working under this captain. Everything was going pretty good. There were certain guys who had gripes—we all did.

So everybody went into the john. We were all standing there in the latrine. Guys were looking in mirrors and walking around. This is where all the talk goes on. That's why they call it "latrine rumors." The rumor factory really was the latrine. Hardly anybody talked about company business down in the day room or the orderly room. It was the latrine.

And so you heard somebody holler from one seat, "Hey, listen, I heard from a guy, a friend of mine down at the battalion headquarters, and let me tell you guys, this is authentic, the real stuff, because this guy works in the department where they cut the orders, he's a mimeograph operator, see. He tells me that we're gettin' this officer from the paratroops. This guy is known as First Lieutenant Bullethead McSnide. He made forty-five jumps in Europe. This guy has got his hair cut so short that he's peeling his skull skin off the top of the bone. And you think this clown we got is bad. Wait till McSnide gets here." And all the guys were saying, "Oh, not Bullethead McSnide!"

Then somebody else said, "Oh, come on, what're you talking about? Don't give me that jazz. Listen, I got a friend down at regimental headquarters. He saw the order, and there's this first lieutenant who used to be a librarian who's being sent. I'll tell you the guy's name." Every time there would be a rumor, guys would make up facts to make them sound better. "Ask me his name, smart guy! McSnide!—ah, who ever heard of him? I'll tell you what his name is, it's First Lieutenant Weathers. And I'll tell you where he is. He's now at McGuire Air Force Base and he's in charge of the library there, and they're sending him here because we're a radar unit and they don't want any of the guys doing PT and getting nervous and then can't watch the radar. It's gonna be great!"

And the other guy would say, "Ah, blow it out! Get outta here! Don't give me that stuff. My friend down at Battalion—." So the words were going back and forth.

Well, thirteen-hundred arrived and everybody was all dressed up for the change of command. All dressed and shaved because you want to make a good first impression. I had my collar all neat and I had my tie tied right, and my jacket was all neatly buttoned, and the whole bit.

And sure enough, at five minutes to the appointed hour we heard the whistles going and there was Kowalski walking around, crummy, rotten Sergeant Kowalski with his hat pulled down and with his green sunglasses. He had this great big clipboard with all the names and I saw our captain come out all dressed up with a big briefcase full of stuff and he brought us to attention: "Prepare to change command, *hup*!" You don't hear that one very often, but it means "Prepare for the worst, men!" He hollered, "Company at ease."

And down the company street came a jeep. Little did we realize, it was fate! Fate in a four-cylinder Willys Jeep. Fate. The avenging angel was approaching—wearing rimless glasses.

Here was this mild-looking officer, a first lieutenant, coming closer. Our captain was standing out there at ease, he had his first lieutenant exec officer next to him, who was being transferred with him. The jeep pulled up in front of the orderly room and out stepped this first lieutenant. And the captain hollered, "Company, atennn-*hut*!" And we all snapped to. What was so great about it was that our officer, who looked like Gary Cooper, looked like the kind of guy who was going to take Burma single-handedly—and as I later understand it, he *did*! He was the kind of guy who would strike terror into the heart of any goof-off. He just looked like the kind of officer who was on the ball all the time. But this new officer had the soft look of a very, very unsuccessful nebbish—which is a great kind of officer to have. White face, rimless glasses, and immediately we thought, this is the guy from the library!

He stepped out of the jeep, walked up to the vaptain, saluted, and the vaptain saluted him. The vaptain turned to all of us and said, "Men, I'm about to turn the command of Company K to Lieutenant Cherry. Now I know that all of you men are going to do your best for Lieutenant Cherry. Lieutenant Cherry is a fine officer and I'm sure he's going to change a few things around here to suit himself. Any good officer does that. I run my company my way and he'll run the company his way. But you're all good men, and I want to say, as I'm about to transfer out…" One of those tear-jerking moments, you know. "I want to say, as I'm about to transfer out of Company K, I want to say to all you men, it has been a pleasure to serve with you. Wherever you men go, whatever battles you men may see, I'll always remember, down in my heart, one of the finest groups of GIs that I've ever had the honor to lead and be part of, was Company K, 362th Airborne Mess Kit Repair Battalion. And now I'm going to turn command over to your new officer. And I want all of you men to give everything you've got to this man. This man comes with a great record behind him and I know that you're all going to be proud to serve under Lieutenant George L. Cherry. Company, atennn-*hut!*"

Somehow, for that brief moment, we felt like we were in the *real* army. We were all standing at attention, the officers were all saluting and Lieutenant Cherry, our new officer, threw us one of those Air Force, snappy salutes—that kind of casual one, and he threw it to our Captain, and our Captain stood straight as a ramrod. He saluted Lieutenant Cherry and handed over the secret Company records. Which, by the way, contained all the various details of all the guys to watch out for, all the rotten guys and all the good guys. He turned and he said, "Good luck, men. Good luck," and he saluted all of us, hopped in the jeep and he and the exec rode out of our lives forever. Down near the battalion headquarters they turned and disappeared. Never again to be seen by Company K.

Well, there we were, all alone. We got a new daddy. How little did we realize how right that would be.

We were all standing there waiting, at attention, and Lieutenant Cherry walked casually up and down the ranks. Just looking. Not saying a word. And trailing behind him was his executive officer, a brand new and spanking second lieutenant with a shaved neck. That neck was red—he was six feet, nine inches tall—a shaved-neck second lieutenant right out of Fort Benning. A couple of crossed rifles on his fatigues, walking along behind the first lieutenant.

Cherry looked into each GI's eyes. Ever have that kind of inspection? That's an eyeball inspection. I remember him looking at me right in the eye. He just looked through those rimless glasses. I looked back. I expected him to say, "Give me the serial number of your rifle, soldier." Nothing. He didn't say a word. He looked at Gasser's eyes. I could hear Gasser's sharp intake of breath. He moved down to Edwards—you could see his knees sagging a little.

He just walked up and down the lines. He finished and he snapped a quick right face, he snapped out to the front of the company, another quick right face, he marched to the middle of the company and he did an about face. And then he hollered out—the first words he spoke to us. "At ease, men. Now mens, I don't know what kind of company that the captain's been running, but my company is different.

"The first thing I want this company to know—that I don't only run a good company—but I run a *beautiful* company. Have you heard that word before, mens? *Beautiful* company. That means that I believe that a man who lives in a place that is beautiful is likely to have a beautiful soul. Look at this company area. From now on I want you to field-strip every cigarette butt you smoke. And any man found not field-stripping a cigarette butt is gonna get busted. And if he ain't got no rank, he just ain't gonna get out of this company area for seven long days. That's number one. Any questions?" What do you say? That is a rhetorical question. Chris Metropolis is not going to say, "Does that include Camels, sir? Or does that only hold for Lucky Strikes?" There was a long, pregnant pause while that was sinking in.

And then Lieutenant Cherry continued, "In addition to that, we are going to draw, as of oh-eight-hundred tomorrow morning, whitewash. We are going to draw brushes, and we are going to whitewash the latrine until not a single knot shows. Not a single nailhead shows. And we are going to continue to whitewash that latrine until that latrine is the whitest, cleanest, shiniest latrine in the entire Camp Crowder area. Corporal, will you please take a note. Tomorrow morning, I want a detail to go down to the QM to pick up ten gallons of whitewash, I will need twenty-five whitewash brushes. I want that detail back here by oh-nine-three-oh. Any questions, mens?" Well, I mean, what do you say to that?

"And now, mens, take a look at them ditches. I want you to look at them ditches around here. Look at them ditches with the weeds growin' in 'em. There will be no beer hall tonight, there will be no going to the service club tonight, there will be no PX tonight, there will be no USO tonight. Starting immediately following chow, at 7 P.M., we are all going to fall out in fatigues and we are going to do something about these ditches. Now, corporal, I want you to provide these men tonight with ten wheelbarrows. If you have to borrow them from regimental headquarters and QM this afternoon, I want you to get 'em. There will be ten wheelbarrows and there will be twenty-five picks. There will be twenty-five shovels, and I want all you men, and I don't care whether you've been on sick call for a week, you're gonna be out here. We will find somethin' for you to do. I want you to wear your dirtiest fatigues. I want you to appear in leggings, helmet liner, fatigues. You can leave your gas masks in the barracks. Any questions?

"Furthermore, corporal, I want you to bring out what white-wash we do have in the supply room for use tonight. If we need any more now, we will send over to Company G and possible even to Company M.

"All right, men, I want to tell you it's going to be a pleasure to be in charge of a company that has such a *fine* reputation as Company K. Now, we're gonna get along fine. I've got one slogan that I've always carried forward in my army career, and that is this. And I want you to listen carefully. You are going to hear this from me. You are hearing it. Are you hearing me? If you play ball with me, I'll play ball with you. Any questions?"

Well, what do you say to that? If you play ball with me, I'll play ball with you! Lieutenant Cherry snapped to attention and the sun was hanging high over the company street. A new era had begun. A new administration had taken office. And all those old, quiet evenings spent in the day room playing pool suddenly had taken leave and flown off over the horizon. Those quiet nights down at the PX drinking 3.2 GI beer had disappeared forever. We were now in a new world.

The company went back to the barracks, and you never saw a more silent group of guys. It had hit with such a thunderclap that we didn't even have time to formulate our griping. It was beyond griping. What are you going to do? Are you going to gripe when a tornado hits? All you do is grab what you can hang on to and hold onto the ground. You don't gripe.

There were guys sitting on footlockers, other guys stretched out on their bunks, two or three guys sat there and scratched their toes, a couple of guys just stood and looked out the windows, other guys down there were spitting in the butt cans. Not a word. Supper went just that way. We sat quietly and ate our SOS, little realizing the enormity of the task we were assigned.

After supper we fell out on the company street and we couldn't believe what we saw. (Our entire company area—and there were a lot of floods in the Missouri area—was sliced up and down with great drainage ditches, maybe eight or nine or ten feet deep. Tremendous ditches that ran all up and down the company streets.) There, set up by every one of those ditches, were night lights for us to work with. There were not only night lights, there was a shiny, beautiful formation of wheelbarrows. And beside each wheelbarrow was a pile of picks and axes. And beside each pile of picks and axes was a duty corporal with his fangs sharpened.

We fell out. Kowalski began to give us our orders. "Lieutenant Cherry said we are gonna go down and we're gonna dig up all them rocks that you find down there by the rifle range and we're gonna bring them rocks back in them wheelbarrows and we are gonna line our company drainage ditches with rocks all the way. We're gonna have the most beautiful drainage ditches in the entire U.S. Army. We're gonna line 'em with rocks and we're gonna whitewash them rocks. Any questions?—No. Okay, line up in a column of twos. The man on the left take a pick and the man on the right take an ax and every fifth man grab one of them wheelbarrows and let's get moving out!

We toiled, we slaved, I was up and down those drainage ditches on my knees carrying rocks. We did this until lights out—until the sound of taps. The next night we did it until lights out and the sound of taps.

And you know, there's a certain maniacal thing about that kind of work. You begin to get interested in it. Has it ever occurred to you that a guy in Sing Sing chopping rocks, making little ones out of big ones, eventually forgets how nutty it is, doing what he's doing, and he becomes an aficionado! He begins to enjoy chopping up rocks. We piled stones on top of stones and we began to be artistic, painting them. Week after week this went on. Every night other companies on their way down to drink beer would look and go *buckbuckbuckbuckbuck*. And we began to have this pride. We had these beautiful, these magnificent white rocks piled up all the way. And what a lovely company we had.

And then one day—out of the blue—it was announced that the major general in charge of the entire Signal Corps was going to inspect the camp! And we stood at attention in front of our beautiful white, our magnificent rock-lined drainage ditches, the only company in the entire camp! And we stood out like a beautiful, shiny new half dollar.

The major general's command car swept up and down the company streets, and all of a sudden he stood up in the back, and I'll never forget this. We were all standing at attention. He hollered, "Whose company is that! Who's putting all them rocks down there by these ditches? Who's the officer responsible? By tonight I want all those rocks taken out of here. This is a *uniform* camp! What is all this? What are they trying to do? Make rock gardens? We're in the army. We're not havin' no rock gardens here! What is this, a ladies' tea party? All right now, move on, captain. And whatever officer who's responsible for this, I want this cleaned up by tomorrow night!"

We spent twenty-four hours taking every rock back to the rifle range, and not only that, washing the whitewash off of every rock—and placing it in the original hole from whence it came. So after eight weeks of Lieutenant Cherry, we were right back where we started from.

Except for one thing. He was in the orderly room thinking up the next project. Hang loose, gang. Things could be worse. Things could be worse. Are you sure you want to transfer out, friend? Things could be worse, you know.

POLE CLIMBING

I'm eighteen years old and they've shunted me from one Signal Corps school to the next, and each one is somehow getting a little more sinister than the last. Each one. I remember the first time I'm working on a piece of equipment and I read the circuit diagram and it says, "This diagram for self-destructive elements." It's got *bombs* in it! Up to this point you've just been taking tubes out and putting them in. You know this thing is all wired to blow up!

Then I tiptoe into the next school. And it seemed such a great one. They said it was a "pole line construction school." That sounds like nothing. Just like labor, doesn't it? Pole line construction school. And everyone said that sounds pretty good. And they picked guys who were in good physical condition. We figured that was for carrying poles and stuff. They gave us physical tests. We ran around and stuff. They said, "We're going to send you to pole line construction school, guys," and so we arrived Friday night in this new school. It was dark. Ever gone to a summer camp where they put you in a cabin or a tent and you can't see the rest of it out there and you suspect something's great out there? The lake, the mountain. It's Friday night.

Saturday morning dawns and we look around. And over on one end of our area is a field. Picture this in your mind. This field is absolutely denuded of every blade of grass. Absolutely flat like a table. They had rolled and rolled it and rolled it until it stretched maybe two miles. Fantastic distance. Just two miles of absolutely bare earth. Not a hill, nothing. But on that bare earth was a solid porcupine fur of telephone poles. Telephone poles sticking up like some insane, surrealistic forest that everyone had stripped the leaves from. Looked like skeletons. Just these white poles. Of all different heights, like a *gigantic* graveyard, stretching out and out and out and reaching up and up. There are little poles and big poles. Now you look at me and say, "What's scary about that?" That's exactly my reaction the first morning. It looks like fun, kind of like gym.

So Sunday passed peacefully. Monday morning arrives, the whistle blew. You know that first day in school, the little tremulous feeling you have—you don't know what's going to happen. You look around. You sort of stand there and you try to be on your best behavior. You don't know about this first sergeant, about this duty sergeant. You're going to play it real cool. You're going to watch and see what happens. That's the big thing in the army. That you learn. Watch and see. Wait! Watch! Keep watching! Keep your eyes open! We're all standing there and the eyes are shifting back and forth.

This guy's walking up and down in front of us and he hollers, "You men are here to learn pole line construction. Any you guys ever done any climbing? Any done any climbing, any a ya?"

Well, all of us have climbed trees. We've all climbed little things. So everybody says, "Yeah."

"No, I mean any *real* climbing!"

Nothing. We're all standing there. Nobody volunteers, we just watch.

"You're gonna be in the charge of Sergeant Abernathy, who's gonna teach you how to climb long-line construction poles. It ain't easy. And some of you guys aren't coming back."

Coming back from what?! He means from that field. He doesn't mean the Germans.

"Sergeant Abernathy, take over." And here comes this angry little man built like a bowling pin, and he clanks when he walks. He's got climbers on. These little iron things with the spikes. He's got a big, wide belt around him that's got pliers, hammers, wire cutters, got big leather gloves attached to it. And he's got a *huge* belt that hangs way down, big silver clips on it and he walks out in front of us, tin hat, snotty little guy. He walks out, says, "All right, you guys, we're goin' down to the dayroom now. We got one hundred fifty sets of climbers and I'm going to show you how to put them on. Follow, let's go. Let's go. Get on the ball. Let's go."

Into the dayroom and they've got all of these things laid out. All these climbers. What is a climber? It's a kind of thing that straps onto your shoes and it has spikes sort of like baseball spikes. There are simple little pieces of our existence that strike terror into the hearts of men, that most other people don't even know about. All of us are afraid of guns. Spears, swords. How many of you know the fear that almost everybody who's ever used a pair of climbers feels when he sees them?

I mean a *real* thick fear? We didn't know it yet. We sort of say, "Hey, Charlie, look. Wow!" We're putting them on. Gee, look! And you put them on and you start walking and it's like wearing baseball spikes. You go clank! Clank! Clank! There's a long spike that sticks out. It's about three inches below your shoe. It's a big piece of metal. There's a belt around, another belt, another belt, and the big spike. You stand there and you've really got a grip, and you walk sort of stiff-legged.

He yells, "All right, you guys, pick up your equipment belts now. Don't ever wear 'em tight. You hear that? They'll tear your gut out!" Tear your gut out! You wear them loose so if you're flying through the air you can get rid of it on the way down! So you don't get stabbed by your own pliers. He yells, "Wear 'em loose! And I want you to practice with that buckle. 'Cause if you start cuttin' out, the first thing you do is throw your safety belt off. Unclip this thing and let go!"

Somebody says, "Sergeant, what's cutting out?"

"You'll find out!"

So we get all prepared. You know, there's a great feeling—all kids have a secret little love of putting things on their bodies. Strapping things on. Little hats and stuff like that. And each one of us shares this. So there's a kind of fun putting these things on. Big pair of wire cutters, here's a tremendous collection of pliers. And it's yours. All new and it's beautiful.

He gets us outside. "All right, men, you're equipped now for pole line construction duty. Don't kid yourself, 'cause you got equipment—you know nuttin'! You don't! About face. Take one step forward in the company street. Right face. Forward harch!"

And we go off. Double time, *clank clank clank clank clank clank* and we're getting closer. The poles are coming. We had been seeing them from about a mile's distance. *Clank clank clank clank clank.* And they're getting bigger. *Clank clank.* The closer we get the higher they get, the skinnier they get. Higher! And suddenly we're here. And we stand.

"All right now, men. I will demonstrate how you take your first hitch on a pole. He goes *clank.* Boom! Zoom! Up he goes! We watch. Have you ever seen those guys on poles? Doesn't it look easy? Doesn't it look like fun?

He yells down at us, "All right now. Watch this." He's up there on the pole and we're all watching him. "Keep your knees stiff! Swing out, lean back on your belt. That belt is not a safety belt, it's a work belt." Everybody felt that if you put the belt on it keeps you up there, but, "That ain't no safety belt, it's a work belt. You lean back, you work. But if you cut out, if them things let go, you get rid of that thing and down you go! Don't hang on! I'll tell you why. You'd reach the bottom of that pole looking like a porcupine. You would have eight-foot slivers that went in here and came out the top of your head.

Good god! All of a sudden it's getting very menacing, this pole we're going to climb. He says, "All you guys in the first row, I want you to take one step forward, harch! All right now, each one of you, address your pole." (That's army talk. It means look at the damn thing!) "Address your pole and upon command, I want all of you to take your right foot, raise it above the left, plant it in, take a short hitch, up and then up, up, up, one, two, three and stop at the third one."

Up to this time telephone poles have just been things you carve stuff on, or you spit at or throw rocks at. All of a sudden this thing's glaring at you. Leering at me. And I can smell the creosote and I can see where millions of other guys have climbed up those holes. They've gone up and the pole is splintered and rotten. This has been climbed on since the first Germans went into Poland. Ten million Signal Corps soldiers have climbed to the top of these things and have looked right over the bull's horns, and climbed down. And now, here I am. I stand there.

He yells, "Right foot—into the pole, heppp." And I'm hanging there. I discover that I've got ankles made of spaghetti. And I'm only three inches from the ground! "All right, left foot up, huppp! Up, huppp!" Ohhh! I'm hanging, oh, oh! "All right, hold on now!" And everybody's tearing and here we're three feet from the ground! And the pole goes all the way up into Heaven somewhere.

"Hold on now. The easy part is gettin' up!" You never think of coming down. It seems so easy. "All right, now, raise your foot straight up, don't bend your ankle." With that I go *pow*! Eight guys out of ten go down on their asses and we're lying there. He says, "All right, you men, get up, get up, you slobs. Do you realize that if you had done that another three feet higher, we'd have the ambulance here?" Yes, yes, I know, I whimper to myself.

Well, this continues for the first morning. And as it continues, the fear builds in and at the same time a peculiar kind of pride builds up. It must be the same thing with guys who walk tightropes. You're scared but you're glad you can do it. And so we begin to climb higher and higher until by the end of the second day we are climbing thirty-foot poles. That's almost three stories. Can you imagine yourself hanging from the top of a tiny toothpick thirty feet up, just hanging there with the story ringing in your ears of "cutting out." The wind is blowing, back and forth, back and forth.

He says, "Look, we're gonna work on the thirty-foot poles two straight days. Then we're gonna climb! Then we're gonna *climb*!" We think, let's stop here, we're pretty good!

And on the fourth day we arrive at what they call the major pole area. These poles range from forty-five feet to ninety-six feet in height. Have you ever seen a ninety-six-foot-high pole? Oh, my god! They're made out of wood, the same kind of wood. They're not much thicker than the others. It's like climbing up a string—almost ten stories. Well, on the fifth day we're beginning to develop this thing inside. We *hate* to get out there. You know the terrible fear that you have of failure? You want to stay in bed? By Thursday it's almost impossible to get us up. We all pretend we're tired. But every day we get these things and start putting them on. Because you know it had to happen. You just know something had to happen.

We're now working on the sixty-footers. Sixty feet is roughly five stories or above. And about three o'clock in the afternoon I have worked my way up to the top of a sixty-foot pole. And I'm looking down. That's one of the great commandments: "Don't look down!" Stop looking down. And immediately you look up. Have you ever looked up from sixty feet? Boy, those clouds are going by and a bird goes past you and he's *under* you. You're hanging up on this pole and you keep saying to yourself, "Don't look down, don't look down, don't look down." You're sixty feet up and the wind goes *woooooooo*! You're swaying a full two feet back and forth and you look down, you're way over there and you're way over here and you can hear your climbers creak and way down below I can hear the sergeant, "All right, you guys come on down."

And I start going down. I made about three steps down, and you know, you figure you're pretty good. About three steps, and suddenly I hear a *rip*! A ripping sound! Just like somebody ripping a pair of Levi's. And I feel something happen. A funny feeling in my left foot. I just feel it and I dig my right in, and my left foot is floating free. It had cut out. I put it back in and I start working it. I get it stuck in solid. I'm sweating like a pig, hanging on and wind is blowing past me. Swaying back and forth. Now everything goes! You know what happens when you get scared? Everything you've learned goes out of your head. Gone, gone, gone! You become a basic animal, and all it says, that basic animal, is, "Hang on, hang on, don't move!" I'm hanging on and I look out and see the other guys are going down and I hear, "Come on, Shepherd!"

So I start working my way down and I get about halfway down when suddenly I hear floating up to me, this strange sound—like a faint siren. It just went *waaaaa* and I heard a silence. And I knew somebody had fallen. It wasn't me. I knew somebody had gone. It's a terrible moment and I don't know whether I should look down or what. I start working down and I hear a lot of talk down there, a lot of guys running around, and I'm working my way down.

And it's the sergeant who hollers, "Shepherd! Stay where you are. Don't move. He could see that I was chicken. I'm hanging there. I peek down and I see about thirty guys all around the base of a pole. And there is that little tiny figure. And I see the jeep coming over the field and I can see that big, white wagon with the big red crosses coming over the field. And I'm hanging there. Just hanging. That wind's blowing. Way off over in the distance is the Ozark Hills that you hear those folk songs about. And I'm hanging. Looking. They pick this guy up and he isn't moving. I can see he's just all limp. Into the wagon and off they go.

And then it comes. The sergeant yells up. "Shepherd! You want me to come up after ya?" Do you want me to come up after ya? They really do say that. They get very scared when there's a casualty on the climbing field. They absolutely panic because everybody else goes down—it's like one guy falls and the rest come down like leaves. You loose all your guts, your knees get weak and down you go! And you're forty feet up, you know, you come down like a rock! So I say, "Nooooooo!" *Ohhhhhhh*! And I start edging down and I keep thinking to myself, keep your knees stiff. Now one, two, down, down, down, and I'm working my way down, down, down. And I finally touch the ground. Good god! And I stand there and nobody's paying any attention to me. I'm down. I walk, I clink a little bit, I'm at least ninety years old. I go walking over to the rest of the guys and they're sort of talking around, taking a ten-minute break.

And they do not allow you to dwell on the last crash. So everybody finishes his cigarette and the sergeant says, "All right now, address your pole. We are carrying aloft crosstrees. Pick up your crosstree." We've been practicing how to attach the crosspiece to the top of a pole, but this is the first time we've ever done it on the top of a high pole. So I begin to climb. And each step I'm getting more scared. And I can hear the sergeant running back and forth down there. "All right, keep on moving. All right, boys." He knows we're all up there scared. "Come on!"

And about halfway through climbing up, the sergeant suddenly hollers, "Halt!" We're swinging in the wind, each with a cross-pole. I look over and about thirty-five feet up, one of the GIs has frozen. He's hysterical. He's busted. And he's just hanging on there. He's frozen. And he's crying, he's yelling. And all of us, each one of us, eight million monkeys in the trees and one monkey's flipped his wig. We're all hanging there and he's screaming. And the sergeant yells, "Go on up, you yellowbelly. Get up there."

And the guy continues to cry. And the sergeant yells, "All right, I'm comin' up after you." And he starts to climb up like a fiend! And this kid is looking down and he starts climbing again, with the sergeant after him. The kid gets to the top and here we all are now, a hundred and twenty guys with cross-poles at the top of enormous telephone poles sixty feet in the air.

And the sergeant goes back down and yells at us, "All right now. Attach those poles and have them attached in forty-five seconds. I'm timin' ya. When I give the go, go! GO!!!" And we start sweating up there, taking the bolt out. Oh, it's terrible when you have to let go in order to get the bolt out. *Ohhhhh*! The cross-pole is like the wing of a big airplane—and the wind! Sixty feet up. *Ahhhh*! *Ohhhhh*! Oh my god! But I've got it tight and I start climbing down. About thirty feet on the way down I feel like I've made it. I'm a pole linesman. I'm climbing down and I'm about halfway down the pole and I look two poles over at Gasser, my old buddy, and I say, "Come on, Gasser!" And suddenly, *oooomf*! I am in midair. And that instinct went just like a clock—detach that belt quick, man! And I hit it and *doinggg*! It says to kick away from the pole and I am going down.

The next thing I know I am in the clinic. It is ten days later and I see above me these little metal poles with all these little pulleys, these winches. I'm lying there and it was just like someone turned the light out. It's just now, all of a sudden, light. I didn't come out gradually, I just came out. It's like I'm still on the sixty-foot pole. I didn't feel a thing.

A girl comes over, a second lieutenant who's a nurse. She looks down at me and says, "How are you, mac?" It's the army, you know.

And I say, "What happened?"

"You'll be all right." She walks away.

And I can see out the window, way off in the distance, the tops of the poles. Just out there in the distance. And about ten minutes after I can hear them coming down the ward. I can hear my buddy, Gasser, coming.

Gasser says, "How are you, Shep?"

And behind me is the sergeant who is looking down at me, and what he says to me is, "How are you, Shepherd? Keep your knees tight!"

~~~~~~~~~

We were all down on the ground. We were standing there. All of us except one man. The guy who wouldn't climb the pole. And that little corporal grabbed him by the collar. He said, "All right now, I want all you to watch this. I want every last one of you to watch this now. There ain't gonna be no chicken soldiers in my outfit. Now you come over here with me."

He yanked this guy across the street where they had a pole set up that must have been fifty feet high. A big baby just standing up there and it had a crossbar on top of it with a pulley. He attached to this guy's waist, a belt. And he said, "You hang on to that rope, now here we go." With that, four guys were detailed to haul him up hand over hand. He is out of his mind. He is one of the few people who has a genuine, psychological fear of heights. And they just kept cranking it up and up and up until there he hung, four stories in space. Screaming. Spinning round and round and round as the wind blew him back and forth like a pendulum.

We are all standing there watching him and our climbing irons are digging deeper into our ankles, digging deeper into our kneecaps, and he's swinging back and forth up there. And all of a sudden you can see he's sick and he throws up and it comes flying down through the air.

That little old corporal hollers, "And when you've got enough, when you're ready to climb, you just let me know, buddy. You just let me know when *you're* ready to climb. And you are gonna hang there until you lemme know, got it? You answer me! Don't you get smart with me! I'll leave you hanging there till you let me know."

Well, that guy hung there for three hours while we moved from pole to pole and climbed. All the while he spun as the wind swung him back and forth. And then, finally, maybe about five or five-thirty, half an hour before mess time, we all lined up and our first sergeant marched us away into the darkness. We all could see as we marched in the darkness, behind us was that soldier, swinging back and forth, four stories in space. And that little corporal standing down there below. You could hear his voice as we marched away: "And you just lemme know when you're ready to climb, mac. I got all the time in the world."

Just one of the great moments. One of the great, singular moments. And those poles stood there outlined against the sky, just cold, white, dead trees against the dark background like some Japanese forest that had lost somewhere the branches, the leaves, and the life.

SERVICE CLUB VIRTUOSO

I'm in the army—the first moment that I ran into true folk talent. A true folk talent. I'm a kid, you know, I came from Hammond, Indiana where nobody worries about art—if you take accordion lessons, you take accordion lessons, that's the end of it. If you take tap dancing lessons, that's called art. If you take steel guitar lessons and learn to play "Aloha" or "Honolulu Nights," or something like that, that's what kids did. They all went at the age of six to somebody's "accordion emporium" down at the end of the street and they took accordion lessons and became part of an accordion band.

One of the more frightening things that I've seen in my life was seventy-five kids in an accordion band, all together, playing "Red Sails in the Sunset" on four-hundred and ninety-five-dollar accordions. Oh, what a scary thought that was! Being paid for by guys working nights in the blast furnace. Now, I'm not sure what they thought they were *paying* for. That's an interesting question when you stop to think about it. I guess, in Hammond, Indiana, they thought they were introducing their kid to art. And the kid, sitting there with that great big sequin-encrusted accordion with his name, "Jimmy," on the front of it. And he's pumping out "When the Swallows Come Back to Capistrano." That was considered art.

That was the crowd, too, who believed that Nelson Eddy was a magnificent opera singer. And their idea of what they call classical singing was Jeanette MacDonald and Nelson Eddy singing excerpts from "The Chocolate Soldier." "Tramp, tramp, tramp, the boys are marching!" That kind of thing. It was very serious classical music and they'd get all dressed up in their Sunday suit to go hear it at the Grant Park Shell. This is the background that I came from.

So I'm in the army and I'm about eighteen years old and I've just gotten started in this whole mess. They've given me rifles and I've got pistols hanging all over me and I've become dynamic. One of the scariest things was to arrive at camp and spend about eight weeks on the obstacle course. You ought to crawl through those on a hot August day for about eight hours straight. You get to see the bottom of civilization after a while. Falling down over cliffs, and culverts all stretched out in a line, water running through them. And it isn't only water they're running through them. They've got the camp runoff, all the stuff—to give you your training in what the real thing is. It's real! You're slogging along through this stuff with your pack. And your new equipment is wet and your face is wet and the wind is blowing and the dust is flying into your ears and you come crawling out into another blast of heat and up you go up the rope ladder, over the top, and your pack is hitting you in the back of the head and the helmet is ringing in your ears and your canteen is—I still have a permanent groove right down here where the canteen got me. It was always getting me. And your gas mask—I have a flat rib over here where the mask got me. On I go, over the cliff.

After a while it's weirdly funny. One day I'm standing in the latrine shaving. They have eighty-five mirrors, and looking out at me is a totally different guy! The kind of guy that, just a year before, had I seen this guy in a diner, I would have nudged Flick in the elbow and said, "Watch out for that son of a gun." And there I am, a square-jawed, angry-looking, arrogant, rotten person. And I'm standing there shaving this face. And it's me! I'm looking out and I'm swearing. All of a sudden I'm one of those guys—every second word is a single, army, all-purpose, universal solvent. The army has a single word that it uses to solve all problems. And don't think for a minute I don't use it. Ike was in the army and Ike must have hollered that same word into the phone. He says, "What? Montgomery said what?! Well, you tell him…" *Pow*! Don't think he didn't. And I know for a fact Truman did. Absolutely. In fact, I never knew a guy in the army who didn't.

There's eighteen million shadings on this word. So here's this guy—I'm shaving myself, I'm looking at that thing in the mirror and I'm saying these words as these guys keep walking in, "Flawaawaawaa!…" "Ah, come on, Shepherd, will you *flawaawaawaa*? How long you gonna use the sink?" Eight guys are lined up behind me. And I'm the same guy that, had I gone into the diner the year before and seen this lout up there where the donuts are, paying the waitress, the same, I'd have kicked Flick in the shins, my buddy, and said, "Let's keep an eye on that son of a gun, he's gonna jump anyway, he's gonna steal the Ford." There I am, shaving this thing. That's the way it is.

That's what they call indoctrination. I'll never forget the first moment. I'm not in the army eight minutes when there's a guy standing up in front of us and he's got a film going. It shows a lot of Germans flying over Rotterdam and stuff, and he stops the film. This colonel comes out and he says, "We're gonna turn you guys into (blankin') killas!"

Well, so I'm sitting down there, I'm fresh out of Miss Shield's Sunday school class. All right, let's see you do it to *me*, mac. And, by George, not more than eight weeks later, what do you think I am? "A (blankin') killa!" I'm shaving it. This rotten-looking face—a thing! Sure, it's a long time ago, it's over four hundred years I'm talking about, but it has never gone away! Once you've turned into a blankin' killer.

So I'm standing in front of the mirror and I'm shaving this rotten-looking face that's me. Square-jawed, I've got those little veins on the cheekbones, and my eyes are bloodshot from running into those great big things with the rope ladders all day long. You know what happens when you start using that kind of language continually like you use in the army—you begin to look like the language. They say that language forms people, and you can't separate it. Well, if you've only got one word in your entire vocabulary, you are formed, boy. I turn around to those guys waiting for the sink and I holler my favorite word, "*Flawaawaawaa!*" And they holler their favorite word back. Every time I cut myself I holler my favorite word. Every time I reach down to put a little more shaving cream I holler my favorite word. I turn the water on. Out comes cold water—no more hot water so I holler my favorite word. The plug is leaking and the water's going out and I holler my favorite word. And then, finally, when I finish, I wipe my face off and somebody says, "Come on, get going!" I holler my favorite word.

I turn around and go back into the barracks, I start putting my shoes on, I bust my shoelace—guess what I say. So, after all, you get to be the same kind of guy, and it has never left me. I'm afraid you never completely expunge the roots of your childhood— which I spent in Camp Crowder. You never completely expunge it from your soul. Never!

You've got the scene, see, the one-word vocabulary. Everybody's got it. And it sticks with you along with your earlier background of Nelson Eddy and Jeanette MacDonald and accordion bands. So this day, Shepherd is walking down the company street and it's one of those sunny days and everything is working out pretty good. I've got my fatigue hat at a cocky angle that you wear when you're off fatigue, and out of the dayroom comes the lout of a duty corporal and he nabs me. "Hey, Shep. Hey, you, comere, you. Comere. Straighten that cap! Where you goin'?"

I turn around.

He says, "Comere, you go down to the club down there. They got plenty of work for guys like you what don't wear your cap right. I'm gonna call the lieutenant down there to make sure you get there. You tell the lieutenant you need some work. Now get goin! *Flawaawaawaa.*" He hollers that single word.

Oh, nuts, for crying out loud! Down the street I go. I'd been heading for the supply room where Gasser was piling up Form-30s and shoes and stuff. He's got great duty being assigned there where you stand around and smoke cigars and steal field jackets. He sees me going past. "Where you going?"

"I'm going down to the service club."

"What do you mean? They'll catch you down there."

"They already caught me. I'm going down to empty butt cans." (Now you're hearing about the real army.) Down the street I go. Down there at the end of that long, rotten-looking, dreary street, like a depressed area, is the club. "The club" is purely a euphemism. This is not the New York Athletic Club. This club is a great big wooden shed with a wavy wooden floor, and every second week these fat girls from Neosho, Missouri, are trucked in to dance with the first sergeants.

The rest of us are allowed to sit around where they have the typewriters that you put the dime in so you can write a letter home. We're allowed to sit up on the track around the edge and watch them. It isn't a real club. It isn't hard to get in, actually. There are no membership rules. You just have to be completely below the rank of everything to be allowed in.

Now I've got to submit myself to ridiculous stuff, further indignities like clean the butt cans or wash the piano. They have an old piano that had been donated. You know, during the War people are giving away books and stuff—so somebody had a rotten old piano in the basement. "Let's give it to the army." Well, the army got it. One of those great big uprights that hadn't been tuned since the fall of 1908.

I walk into this place. I see nobody. It's empty. Not even the lieutenant in charge of this hovel. And all of a sudden I'm hit—I hear this tremendous sea of sound. *BRABRADAABRAAAAABABAAA!* It's just roaring. The whole place is filled with fortissimo. Remember, I come from the Nelson Eddy world, where a real serious singer like Dennis Day is very serious because he has a high voice. All sopranos are serious classical singers, even if they're singing "Yes Sir, That's My Baby." And here this sound is rolling out and going like mad! Like eighteen pianos pounding out at once. *BRABRADAABRAAAAABABAAA!* *BRABRADAABRAAAAABABAAA!*

I look around, and way down at the end of this long, gym-like affair, in the gloom, is that piano, and I see bobbing up and down behind it, another fatigue hat. And what is he playing? He's playing Gershwin's "Rhapsody in Blue." *BAM-BAMMM-BA-BADABOM-BAAA! BOM-BOM-BOOM-BADABADABADABADA-BOMBOMBOMBOOOM-BAAAA!* He's playing it five times faster than I've ever heard it played before. With at least eighteen thousand more notes than I ever heard before *BADABADABADABADA-BOMBOMBOMBOOOM.* He's playing the whole piano at once, it's going like mad, the piano's bouncing up and down and the hat's joggling up and down and the sweat's flying.

I come closer and all you can hear is this enormous piano going. I'm fascinated. Now remember, friends, I'm talking about "folk talent." I go around the back of the piano and there it is, it's bouncing up and down and the windows are rattling *BAM-BAMMM-BA-BADABOM-BAAA! BOM-BOM-BOOM-BADABADABADABADA-BOMBOMBOMBOOOM-BAAAA!* Boy, he's really belting it out.

I go around the edge of the piano and there's this guy with a receding chin and protruding teeth and he's got a bulging forehead and black, sweaty hair, and he's only about five feet six, his feet barely touching the pedals, he's got a sweaty, rotten stinky set of fatigues, and his fatigue hat's bobbing on top of his head. And he is all over that keyboard simultaneously.

I stand there and look at him and he says, "Hi." *BAM-BAMMM-BA-BADABOM-BAAA!* His arms are flying, his feet are pedaling. I say, "Wow!" All I could say was "Wow!" And he stopped. Crash! *BA-BADABOM-BAAA!* The keys are jiggling and vibrating and the whole piano is going *do-oing-oing-oing-oing-oing!*

He turns around, he's breathing heavy. He says, "You here on duty? You on fatigue with me?"

I say, "Yeah, let's empty the butt cans."

He says, "Okay, let's go. You start at the front, I'll start at the back." So he starts emptying the butt cans and he's emptying like mad!

I'm going slow like one does in the army, you fool around, walking with one butt. And he's running around like mad, and I say, "Hey, come on, take it easy, will you?"

He says, "I want to get back to the piano!"

I say, "All right, all right."

He finishes his half and he runs around, he's back at the piano again, and this time he starts *BA BA BA BAAAAM! BA BA BA BAAAAM!* He's playing Beethoven's "Fifth Symphony." Fantastic roar of sound! And Beethoven's "Fifth" is not piano music, but it is when he's playing it!

So I go up to him and I say, "Come on, wow! Where did you learn to play the piano?"

He's playing like mad. *BA BA BA BAAAAM*! He says, "I just picked it up." *BA BAAAAM*!

He says he just picked it up! I say, "You mean…," hollering over the scherzo movement, "you mean…" *BA BA BA BA BA BA BA BA BA BA BA BA*. He's playing four thousand notes! "What do you mean you just picked it up?"

BA BA BA BA BA BA BA BA BA. He yells, "I play by ear."

I'm staggered. Back home, Mrs. Bruner next door played by ear. Mrs. Shields, our second grade teacher played by ear and her idea of "by ear" was "Twinkle, Twinkle, Little Star" with one finger. That was the era when every radio station had an advertisement that began, "In just seven minutes a day you will be able to play…." and here's this guy who plays Beethoven's "Fifth" by ear! He plays it by ear! I say, "What do you mean by ear? How do you learn that way?"

He says, "I just wanted to play the piano and I sit around and listen to records and the radio and I just play by ear, that's all."

"Do you have anything else you can play?"

He says, "Yes, what would you like to hear?"

"Let's see. I don't know. Anything."

"Well, how about this?" He bats the keys a bit. I never saw a guy play with such gusto! Without any inhibitions he just hits those keys. *BA BA BA BA BA BA BA BA BA*. And he's playing something else.

I say, "Is that the piano part?"

He says, "No. I just play all the parts together."

By now the lieutenant has come in. All lieutenants, in my experience, like to pretend that they have more culture than the EM. They know about things like books and stuff. The guy's playing "Rhapsody in Blue" again, so the lieutenant hollers, "Hey, that's Ravel, isn't it?" Then the lieutenant says, "Wait a minute, wait a minute, wait a minute. Wow," he says. "What a lot of piano! I'm sitting in the office and it's coming in. You're not playing the piano part, are ya?"

The guy gives him a funny look. "Well, yeah, I'm playing the piano."

"But you're not playing the piano *part*." The lieutenant says, "You know, there's a piano part to that music and you're not playing it."

"What do you mean I'm not playing the piano part?" It's a revelation to him! Here's a true folk artist.

The lieutenant says, "You're playing the whole orchestra." He's playing all the notes he hears on the record—the oboes, the flutes, the bassoons. He hears everything else going and to him, that's the tune!

The lieutenant says, "Well, play that over again."

"Okay." He goes *BAM-BAMMM-BA-BADABOM-BAAA*! Four thousand notes come pouring out. Yes, he's playing the entire orchestra. A great folk artist.

For the six months we knew each other before we were both transferred out, once in a while we'd be sitting in the mess hall and somebody would say, "Hey, why don't you play Hayden's 'A Hundred and Second' for us, with all the variations, huh? Why don't ya?" He'd sit there and laugh. I guess that's the only time he realized that he shouldn't be playing the piano that good.

I guess he's long gone from the army, and now he's probably taking simple piano lessons, starting all over again, and he's probably very rotten, playing things like "Twinkle, Twinkle, Little Star," and he can't even remember his army days when he was this great folk artist playing it too wide and too tall and too big, when he was playing it too much.

FOURTH OF JULY IN THE ARMY

I was in this place. And I suddenly found that I wasn't what I had thought I was. I'm going to tell you a very embarrassing story about the Fourth of July. It's an army story. When guys get into the Army or into college or into some kind of gang situation, the general attitude is to put everything down. If you're in college you put down whatever college you're in: "Oh, don't give me that Joe College jazz!" In the army it's also a tradition to put down the army, the United States, everything. There's no thing in the army such as patriotism except at strange, odd moments. It's a very strange feeling, living in twentieth-century America. You're torn between being a Babbitt on the one hand (which we all are, underneath it all), a kind of a herd animal that moos, chews stuff, hollers, and goes bowling. You're torn between that and the intellectual you which, in a sense, is against all of this. Rarely do you ever go completely over from one side to the other. There are large numbers of cross-currents because there are guys from everywhere in the army.

I was sitting in the barracks. Me and Gasser and Zinsmeister, and a whole bunch of guys from Tennessee and some guys from northern Wisconsin and other places. About half of the outfits in this camp had gotten passes for the Fourth of July and were gone. The other half of us were in camp. But they announced that there was going to be nothing doing except a big parade for the people of the little towns near this place. We knew one thing—that the crowd would be coming in, thousands of people would be going past the barracks to watch. The army was going to bring them in buses—chicks and all kinds of people wearing white coats. It was summertime and we were in the barracks sitting in the heat.

It was hotter than blazes because this was out in Missouri and the sun just rocks down and you could smell all kinds of stuff in the heat. You could smell mud, you could smell catfish, you could smell the river, smell the rocks heating up. And barracks had a particular smell anyway, cigar butts that had just been thrown in the butt can, which was down there at the end. You know what is it a butt can—it's a big empty fruit can that's nailed to one of the posts down at the end. Also a very clean sort of strong GI soap-smell because they had a GI party every five minutes and you were scrubbing it all down. This day especially, it smelled like a combination of shoe polish, Blitz cloths, and the clean, pressed fatigues and the suntans for the parade. You could smell it all.

Have you ever been in a parade? I don't mean the kind that just marches down the street. I mean a real, genuine, absolutely all-out, going-the-whole-way parade. We were in the barracks and that afternoon we were going to have the parade.

The parade was to be at one o'clock. It was now about ten. They told us we had the morning off to get our equipment ready for the big parade. Sitting in the barracks the guys were very cool, cleaning their leggings, guys polishing shoes, polishing brass. Yelling back and forth. Everybody was complaining. The whole point is to complain before you go out on a parade. Whether or not you want to is beside the point. It's part of the tradition to refer to it as bullshit. The word is used even more when guys are about to do something exciting. Because this is part of the coolness. You have to go opposite to what you really feel.

I had been appointed guidon bearer, one of the very rare things I had ever been appointed to in the army. Guidon bearer is the guy who marches with this big flag on a staff. They'd taught me how to hold this thing. It goes in a sort of a socket that hangs from a belt around your waist. This is a fantastic flag, it's a floating, silken flag with gold fringe all around the edges of it and tassels hanging down from the gold eagle on top of the staff. A very high-class flag, one of those huge flags they use especially for parading. So I was making snide remarks. "Hey, Charlie, you say you want to polish your shoes?" That kind of thing. You know how guys are. I was flubbing around with this guidon thing—it had a case on it, one of those things that flips down over the top of the flag and the pole, and up to this point it had been in its case.

It was now about twelve-thirty and we were dressed, and they had issued special parade stuff, especially for the guidon bearers, guys who march out in front and march in the back—the various outriders who were given white belts and white leggings. We were all told to wear all of our insignia and stuff—everything—we had hats with the little buttons all over it, buttons on the collar, and all our patches on. The whole jazz. But absolutely we had to be clean and pressed and shined. We were ready and we started to drift out into the company street. I got out there and there was the first sergeant wearing his sunglasses. Sharp! Oh boy, was he ready. There are very few things that look more official, and in a strange way, have such a peculiar beauty, as a first sergeant's set of stripes creased right down the middle like a knife. Usually the stripes go from the guy's arm all the way down to his elbow—great big fat things lying on each side.

The sergeant was out there and he was lining us all up. "All right, you, let's go, you guys." And they were yelling and hollering and blowing their whistles and we started falling in. Shepherd fell in over there to the right of the company with his guidon. And the sergeant hollered, "Cover off, Shepherd, come on, let's go! We're gonna move out here in a couple of minutes. Come on, let's go." So I took the guidon down and Gasser helped me slide the cover off, and I put the staff up and the flag started to float out there. Just a slight breeze caught it—a puff of wind—*wushhhhhh*! It tugs, you know, it's a funny thing about a flag. It sort of tugs against you. You can just feel it moving against you, tugging away.

They blew the whistle and we started to move out. We did a right face and we moved out down the company street in the general direction of the parade ground that was like a huge football field. Grandstands had been set up with bunting, and all the people in them had been given souvenirs and all kinds of little flags and little hats they were all wearing, all along this wall of red, white, and blue bunting. And there was, of course, the reviewing stand, and there was the mayor of this little crummy town wearing a high silk hat, probably the only high silk hat in Southern Missouri. A high silk hat and a cutaway coat. And that sun was beating down. Boy, it was coming down. Just rocking down, about a hundred and twenty degrees, and a slight, steaming-hot breeze moving across. You could hear kids crying and all sorts of little noises in the crowd.

There must have been close to seven or eight thousand soldiers all lined up back of the grandstands. Thousands of us all lined up in our battalions and regiments and companies. We were in the second outfit, and I could see way up ahead of us this brigadier general in front. He was commanding with a sword and the whole business! With a sword! He held the sword up, and all the way down the line the company commanders and the battalion commanders, majors and colonels and captains, were all wearing their swords and straps and absolutely summer-parade best. I've never been in anything like that before or since!

We were lined up behind those grandstands and ready to go. And standing there behind me was Gasser, and we were all putting down the whole thing: "Oh, come on!" Snide remarks like, "Greasy kid's stuff. Ah…" And "Ah, look at the one in the pink dress—wow!" We were looking at the stands and nobody was paying any attention to the lineup.

And way up ahead, off to the edge of the parade ground, not marching, but ready to fall into the column, was the band. They had a big band that had been recruited from the entire Second Army. It had guys from bands that had been in the business for years. A really good band. They had a special kind of uniform with crossed white belts on the front. You could see some orange flags and you could see the sousaphones catching the sun. A huge, beautiful band.

Way over to the edge of the parade grounds was the reviewing stand. On it was the secretary of the interior and there was a full, four-star general—General Summerall—wearing the kind of uniform you rarely see today in the army except under very certain conditions. He was wearing high riding-boots and he had campaign ribbons that went from his collarbone all the way down to his waist. That kind of stuff. All the way! He just looked like a gigantic fruitcake. All over his front there, like a big salad. And he was standing up there straight as a rock, and we could see—"That's a four-star general!"—Stars flashing in the sun, and he was flanked by a couple of brigadiers and a major general and the whole bit! It was wild!

By this time we're getting to have a funny feeling in our stomachs. It isn't exactly what we thought it was going to be like. We're standing there at attention. And suddenly we hear in the distance this hum—*gruuuuuuuum*—there is an artillery battalion over there to the left, way beyond the woods, and they go *pahooooom*! *pahooooom*! And you can hear it echoing. We straighten up. *Bahuuuum*! And then it goes *pchoooooo*! They fire another one. You can see the smoke rising and once again you hear it echoing from the foothills of the Ozarks. You hear it coming back. And this hum is going *gruuuuuuuum pahooooom*! Another one going. And you hear all the guys—the rattling of their straps and their rifles, they're getting slightly tighter and a little straighter. Straightening up their rifles—their Enfields and their Garands and their Springfields, all highly polished, and all the time we are standing at attention. We are waiting to go. And directly ahead of me is our captain, standing like he has been molded out of ebony. Just standing there straight up with his sword.

Gruuuuuuuum, you hear it getting louder and louder, and then—we see, out of the corner of our eye, as we're all trying to stand at attention—out of the corner of our eye we see these things coming in the sky and there is a fantastic formation of B-17s and above them is a flight of P-51s and below them is a flight of P-38s and you just see them coming in and they go roaring over the field at about three or four thousand feet. *Gruuuuuuuum!* And all the while the artillery comes in *pahooooom! pahooooom! pahooooom!* And the planes go off over the hills.

Then we hear a high-pitched *prrrrrrrrrrrehhh*—the whistles go and the band starts to play! You can hear them playing in the distance. I don't know if you've ever been in a parade—and if you are part of it, see—and you hear a really good military band playing from about a half a mile away so at first it just comes to you faintly. And also you can hear way down, those planes going off in the distance and once in a while you can hear coming from the hills just a vague echo of those fantastic artillery barrages. And we start to move out.

We are moving out against the wind. My flag catches the breeze and moves out behind me! It's pulling against me! And the band is playing and I can hear those guys marching and I can hear their canteens rattling behind me. It's insane!—All of a sudden we are marching!—it's wild!

We're going down to the end of the parade ground. A gigantic column left! Column left *rump rump rump rump*. We make that big column left and the band falls in behind us. Great Scott! We are now marching right down the middle of the parade grounds. Millions of people are cheering *ahhhhhhhhhhhhhhhhhhhhhhhhhhhh*! And then from behind us you can hear the sound of those planes coming back *grhrrrrrrrrrrrrrrrrrrrrrrrrrr*. *Booooooooommm*! The artillery again! We marched right down the middle of that field. I want to tell you, the sun beating down, we march down the middle of the field with the general standing there in front of us throwing salutes, our eyes straight ahead and the old band is a-knocking it out. The crowd is cheering, people are waving flags, we can see those hills coming up out there where the rifle range is.

"*Column left, harch!*" And the whole shebang begins a fantastic counter-march. We're cutting through there and my flag is floating a thousand feet above my head. It is an enormous flag, a *gigantic* flag. Next to me is this guy with this great big battalion flag, an enormous orange flag with a big red shield right in the middle of it and in the middle of the red shield is a golden eagle. And under it it says, "*In hoc agricola conc in est spittle lauk, the 3162 over alles.*" And the Signal Corps flag is off to the left flying high with those big crossed flags! That big white one and that big red one! We're marching!

And then, way off behind everything you can hear our trucks going. We have all these great big green trucks, you know—prime movers, full of equipment, full of Leroy diesel engines, full of radar equipment, full of mortar equipment *grrrrrrrrrrrrrrrrrrrrrr*!

So we're making a gigantic left turn *grrrrrrrrrrrrrrrrrrr*! The people are screaming and hollering. And all I can report is that a very funny thing began to set in. When we march the other way we make a great big circle and march right back again in front of the stands, the whole thing going, the flags flying, this general marching out ahead of us. A brigadier general who later became a major general, and I suspect it was because of this day. He is marching, he is holding his sword high above him. You can see it flashing in the sun. He is holding it high, and just as he gets to the reviewing stand, he gives this fantastic salute with his sword! General Summerall throws him a salute! The band roars out!

It was a very strange afternoon. We marched back, down the other way and we got down toward the end and the P-51s, the P-38s, and the B-17s made another big pass over the field and they pulled us all up at attention. General Summerall had a PA system, and I can remember how he talked, because this was a very vivid afternoon for me, and strangely enough, up to this point I had been the biggest put-down artist you ever heard in your life. I was putting the whole jazz down, and I was standing at the end of the field and I had my flag sunk down in that socket and I was braced against the wind, and it was pulling. You're trying to stand at attention while that flag pulls. You feel it rocking you back and forth, and the general started to talk into the PA system. You heard it floating out over the field and bouncing off the hills:

"LADIES AND GENTLEMEN, MEN OF THE 362 SIGNAL BATTALION, THE 3164TH, THE 3167TH, AND THE 813 SIGNAL HEAVY CONSTRUCTION BATTALION, ALL ELEMENTS OF THE 2ND ARMY, I WANT TO SALUTE YOU, AND I WOULD LIKE TO SAY, THIS IS ONE OF THE MOST STIRRING DEMONSTRATIONS THAT I HAVE SEEN IN MANY YEARS' SERVICE TO THE U. S. ARMY."

Well, all of us were standing there and it was hard to tell whether the general meant it. Did the general mean it? It's hard to tell. We were all standing there. You heard the band instruments rattling and you could hear guys flubbing around with the gearshifts in their tanks and stuff. You could always hear vague equipment creakings when everyone was standing there, and the general continued to talk:

"IN THE GREAT TASK THAT LIES BEFORE US, MANY OF YOU MEN WILL NOT BE HERE ONE DAY, A YEAR IN THE FUTURE. MANY OF YOU MEN ARE GOING TO GO INTO THIS WAR AND NOT COME BACK. I HOPE THAT NONE OF YOU MEN EVER REGRET THE IMPORT OF THIS GREAT, HISTORIC CRUSADE. I WOULD LIKE TO SAY THAT I WANT TO WISH EACH AND EVERY ONE OF YOU THE BEST OF LUCK. AND, AS AN OLD SOLDIER, I CAN ONLY SAY, JUST TAKE IT AS IT COMES."

And he was through. He stepped back. What a strange thing to say to us. He stepped back, our brigadier general threw him another salute. You could hear whistles going up and down the line, the band picked up the beat, we made a great left wheel, and we marched back toward the barracks area. We heard people hollering in the background, you could hear the planes disappearing in the distance, you could hear the dishes being washed in the canteen as we marched toward the company area.

Well, we got back to the company area and it was a very strange crew. We arrived in front of the orderly room all covered with dust and sweat, because we'd been standing in the sun for about two hours and that dust, that red Missouri clay, had been rising up around us. I remember very clearly those white leggings, that were very tight, were now covered with a fine red film. You put your thumb on it and you left a big red thumbprint, and the crossed, white leather straps that held that flag were covered with all the strange red dust.

In the barracks we took off our equipment and not a word was being said. Nothing. Just clicks and rattles of belts being unhooked, guys putting stuff away, and you heard guys throwing bolts on rifles, someone blowing out the barrel. Not a word was being said. The whole company was in a completely different mood from before the parade started. There was not one single put-down artist in the outfit. Including me, including Gasser, including all of us. Everybody was completely apart. Nobody saying anything to anybody else because we were all afraid—we were all very embarrassed about how we felt. And how we felt was the very opposite of all the stuff that we'd been saying we felt.

We drifted out into the company street, one by one, and down in the middle of the parade ground, this is what the army had done. I'll always remember this Fourth of July because it was very peculiar—it was a wartime Fourth of July. Immediately after we had marched out, the quartermaster outfit and the engineer outfit had set up about five hundred big, flat tables, and on them the army put its inevitable juice. What it called juice. "The Purple Death," that Kool-Aid stuff. It had it all lined up with big chunks of ice in it, all up and down, on red, white, and blue tablecloths made out of bunting that the quartermaster obviously had been making for two weeks. It had big thirty-two gallon jugs of juice and thousands and thousands of paper cups, with USQM on the side. I never saw paper cups with the quartermaster insignia on it. And they had enormous bologna sandwiches. The only kind the Army knew how to make. Of course they called them something else in the army, which the civilians who were eating them did not know. Tremendous bowls of potato chips—the rubber potato chips that the Army used for amphibious work. Hard and rubbery and they came out of cans.

They had this all laid out and we began to drift back and up to this point we had been told that after the parade we were free—we could cut out and if we wanted to, passes were waiting—we

JEAN SHEPHERD

could go into town. Strangely enough, instead of going into town, everybody began to drift back onto the field. There I am with Gasser, nobody saying anything.

We start to circulate among the tables, among all these people—thousands—it must be the whole town. Must be four thousand people. Guys with freshly-pressed overalls—have you ever seen Missouri hillbillies in town on a Sunday? They wear freshly pressed overalls—they honestly do, and they wear a white shirt under them, and when they're being dressed up, they button the top button. That's dressed up. And they put a little goose grease on the front of their shoes and they put a great big yellow straw hat on. Thousands of these guys walking around. Red-necked guys. Big, fat women in blue aprons. Millions of kids and the most beautiful—I'll tell you, hillbilly girls are unbelievable—the most beautiful—Al Capp was not far wrong, you know. Thousands and thousands of these beautiful hillbilly girls walking around and they are all looking at us like we are seventeen feet tall! Up to that point we had just been rotten GIs who came into town and they would try to take us for everything we had—you know, in the taverns.

And everybody is looking at us and we are walking around with our white leggings and we feel, for the first time, we really feel like we are part of something that everybody not only understands, but in a vague way, *honors. Really honors!*

I'm walking around. I take a big bologna sandwich. Standing around with my hat sort of cocked. We all have our hats cocked fifty times cockier than we should have, pulled down, and all the guys have their brass polished, walking around eating bologna sandwiches. Sort of hanging around. Once in a while , when a lady says something, you're very polite: "Yes, ma'am, yes, ma'am, yes, madam." And I'm wearing my strap with the pouch pulled over to the side, to show that I was the guidon bearer.

"My goodness," a lady says, "that was a very beautiful flag, I can tell you!" These little old hillbilly ladies come up and they say things like, "Say, son, do you happen to know a boy named Caleb? You happen to know a boy named Caleb? That's my son, Caleb. You know Caleb? He was in the camp a couple of months ago, and was shipped to the Pacific. Did you know Caleb Seastrom?"

"No, ma'am, no ma'am."

"Fine boy, and you're certainly a fine boy yourself. That's certainly a beautiful flag you carry."

And the old ladies are walking around and some of them have brought baskets of stuff and are giving guys cupcakes. Cupcakes and cookies. Women out there do that. They bring you jars of blueberry jam and stuff. It's a very unusual scene, memorable scene. All the stuff that I put down. Remember that!

And just about twilight now, it's beginning to get dark and some of the people are getting into their cars and leaving. And just then up over in the hills to the right the army proceeds to fire off probably sixteen million dollars worth of GI-issue fireworks. When the army shoots fireworks off, it really has pyrotechnics. They start off with a bunch of star shells *ptcummmmmmm*! This is the real stuff, you know. This is the stuff that other fireworks imitate. *Ptcummmm*! Drifting down over the hills. *Ptcummmmmmmm*! At this point two P-51s flying at about ten thousand feet come over and drop parachute flares! *Kchooooooooooo*! The flares drift down and everybody is just standing there and it's getting quieter and quieter. Off in the distance the old band is a-playin' and we're all standing around eating our sandwiches and the ladies are drifting in and out, handing us soldiers cookies and cupcakes and jam, and the kids are watching and the big star shells and the sky rockets are going up and it's getting darker and darker and darker.

See, I told you I'd embarrass you.

USO AND A FAMILY INVITATION

I'm sitting in this crummy barracks and there is Gasser sitting next to me, you can smell the butt cans fermenting, and once in a while the squawk box goes "*Auggggg!*" and after that, another obscenity would come out of it. It's connected to the orderly room and there was First Sergeant Kowalski and Captain Cherry. Between the two of them, they were always cooking up these beautiful little things to say. Like, you'd hear "*Auggggg!*" and we'd all cringe. The squawk box! And then it would go, in an electronic blur we could hardly recognize as a human voice, "All of you, on the double!" We'd sit there and look at it, and way down at the end, Edwards, who is the literary one of our crowd, would say some beautiful thing back to the squawk box. It's a two-way squawk box, so you'd hear, "Who said that!?" Silence.

Company K was just trying to make its way through life and this thing comes out of the squawk box, "*Auggggg!* The following men are available for a pass over the weekend and should be prepared to pass an inspection, and here are the men: Shepherd, J. P., Gasser, Edwards." I'm getting a pass! My god, they're springing me! But you always suspect some treachery. Oh, yeah! I remember every time you'd get a pass in an outfit that doesn't give passes, some guys think that means they're preparing you for *something*! One time they took a group out of Company K and we got very nervous, because they posted on the bulletin board, "The following men will have a three-day pass and will obtain transportation home." Everybody said, "Oh, are those guys lucky! How come they rate that?" And three days after they got back from home, they were parachuted into Hungary. Makes you kind of suspicious of passes.

So I'm sitting in the barracks that night and I'm getting a pass! I go down to the orderly room. Me, Gasser, and Edwards, all dressed up, we're going to go out. There's the first sergeant. He says, "All right, you guys, now remember, mens, when you get out of camp, you represent Company K. Remember, mens, Company K's the best damn company in the whole damn army, right?"

Company K, the 362 Airborne Mess Kit Repair Battalion. That's what we always called ourselves. I'm in the handle platoon and Gasser is a cup-man. And don't laugh, because the army travels on its stomach. You see these movies and you see John Wayne jumping out of an airplane. What happens? They land! And they bust up their mess kits. Immediately four thousand other guys come down and they've got soldering irons. Being a service troop is not easy. Nobody sings songs about the Signal Corps. You always hear, "Off we go, into the wild blue yonder." Oh, that bugs us in the Signal Corps! Off we go, into the wild blue yonder! And who's sitting back in that crummy old plane but nine Signal Corps guys who are going to jump down there and lay the communication wire on the battlefield.

So we're in the Signal Corps. And we really have our passes. It's Thanksgiving weekend, I've got my new suntans on, my tie is tied, and I'm prepared. For anything. We go into town, Neosho, Missouri, and you see one hundred and thirty thousand soldiers. The town has a population of thirty-seven hundred, and you see nothing but soldiers. So Gasser, Edwards, and I are now walking around. This is the way it is when you're a GI in town. Walking around looking for something to do, and when everything else has failed, you go to the USO. This is an admission of defeat. And

I'm not saying anything against the USO—you can go there and write letters. And there's nothing like writing a letter on a Saturday night. Very exciting.

And so, after two hours of walking around Neosho, Missouri, walking back and forth looking at the scene, we finally wind up at the USO. Me, Gasser, Edwards. We walk in. There's a couple of sailors and nine hundred Pfcs sitting around. This is like the Sargasso Sea of all the guys that missed out. All sitting there, cursing their luck. Behind the counter at the USO they have a coffee machine and there's a girl giving you free tuna salad sandwiches and in the back there's this tall, skinny lady, who heads the Baptist choir in town and she's playing Ping-Pong with a staff sergeant. It's that kind of life at the USO.

And I have no clue, no way of realizing that I am about to have an educational moment. One of those true, golden nuggets of life. A beautiful one. And one that even years later, I wake up at three o'clock in the morning and I look up at the ceiling and I see the scene again. And I say, "Go, baby! Wow!" Then I really wake up and I see it's New York, nothing old New York, where nothing ever happens like it did this weekend.

I walk up to the counter, and behind the coffee machine is this nice lady. Very nice lady. Flower print dress. Strictly Montgomery Ward. And there's a great philosophical difference between the Montgomery Ward crowd and the Sears Roebuck crowd. It's worse than the Baptists and the Methodists.

I get the coffee and I'm standing there. I've got my new stripes on, Pfc. A great moment. My new stripes on, the first night I'm wearing them out in the town. I'm Pfc Shepherd! I have risen up the command ladder, every inch, clawed my way up. The nice lady says to me, "Young man, would you care to spend a day with a typical Neosho family?"

Well, it depends on the family.

She says, "Would you care to spend a day? We have a policy here at the Neosho USO that we pick a soldier out of every night's group and we invite him to spend the next day with a typical family."

The next day is Sunday in Neosho, and Sunday in Neosho makes Cream of Wheat look like Scotch whiskey, so I figure, what can I lose. She hands me a card that says Mr. and Mrs. A. L. Abercrombie, 422 Main Street.

So I say, "Okay." What can I lose?

I go to the YMCA and sleep the night. The next morning I'm out in the sun as I go along Main Street. The houses are getting neater and neater. More and more frou-frou and swings, and lilacs in front of all the houses. Real Norman Rockwell country. The real thing, apple-cheeked old ladies and everything. I figure this is going to be a drag. I can just feel it coming. There it is, 422 Main Street. And it looks like any other house.

Up I go and knock on the door and I hear footsteps approaching. The door swings open and there in the doorway is the kind of face and body that you only see in the movies that run at two in the morning at the American Legion Hall. She says, "Yes?" That slow, Southern yes. "What can I do for you, soldier?"

"A. L. Abercrombie?"

"That's my mother and daddy. I'm Clarabelle. Come right in."

In I come and this voluptuous doll disappears out another door. Now I don't know what to expect. I cannot *believe* what a classical house it is. This feeling of a really itchy kind of house. Potted ferns and you can hear the aphids. Overstuffed furniture. There's this wallpaper that looks like it's crawling up toward the ceiling, and its got leaves all over it and little cherubs flying. I'm sweating. And there is that smell composed of flowered-print dresses, petrified fig bars, old meat loaves, and Lifebuoy soap, a kind of smell of a grandmother-house.

Out of the back comes Mrs. Abercrombie, and she is incredibly apple-cheeked and grandmotherly. Her hair up in little pins, a little fluffy collar around her neck, and a lavaliere hanging. And she says, "We certainly want to greet you here. We're very pleased. Where did you say you were from, soldier?"

"I'm from..." Where the *hell* am I from? In a situation like this you even forget your name. What am I doing here? This is insane.

She says, "Would you sit down now. Clarence will be here in just a minute. "

And up comes old Clarence. He's got these suspenders, he's got a shirt with a big, solid collar that has a gold button in the back, he's got a big tie, bald head, and he walks in and says, "Welcome, soldier." He sits down opposite me. "Ah was a soldier once."

Oh, not this!

"Yep, Ah'll never forget the time when we went off. How about you and me singing 'Mademoiselle from Armentieres'?"

We sit for a couple of minutes and then Mrs. Abercrombie says to me, "Would you like...Just tell me if you come from a strict family."

I'm thinking of my old man. His underwear open, he's hanging on the refrigerator. Saturday night he's had five bottles of beer. I say, "Yes, he's very strict."

She says, "I don't want to offend you. Now you don't have to do it if you don't like, but I know it is Sunday. But would you like a little glass of sherry wine?"

Well, one of my little secrets is that at my young age, I had only recently made the transition from Coca Malt to Ovaltine. In fact, my idea of a really raunchy drink is a Coke with an aspirin in it, which is supposed to get you bombed!

So I say, "I think I would like a little glass of sherry." She's holding this cut-glass decanter and she pours me a glass and I drink it.

Old Clarence, sitting opposite me, says, "If you don't mind, soldier, as one old soldier to another, you don't mind if I have one myself?"

I say, "No, go ahead."

He pours himself some and we sit there drinking sherry. And we drink some more. And we drink some more, and all the while it's getting hotter in this place and I can't figure out why. I've got this lake of drugstore sherry down inside me going *glug*!

And now it's dinner time and we go into the dining room. Very politely we sit down at the dinner table which has a lace tablecloth and there are dishes with gold leaf all around the edges, and little painted leaves and grapes on them.

Clarence is beginning to act kind of funny, and he says, "And now, I think we'll say grace." He pauses. "No, I don't think we will. How about just digging in!"

We start digging into the fried chicken, and in comes Mrs. Abercrombie with a big bowl of candied yams and stuff, and she sits down and begins to pick at her food. And I'm wondering where that chick is! All I can think of is, where is Clarabelle?

Clarence and I are opposite each other and Mrs. Abercrombie looks up from next to him and says, "Call me Emily."

I say, "Okay, Emily."

She says, "That's nice. I've always wished that I had a son."

Yeah, I've heard that before. We continue eating. Finally we finish, and Emily says, "Did you enjoy the sherry?"

"Yes, I sure did," I say.

"How would you like a little of the *real* stuff?"

Clarence says, "Bring it out, Em."

Emily goes to the cupboard and brings out a jug. Little do I realize that the stuff is to be my first meeting with Missouri white lightning. She says, "After all, it is Sunday, and I'm going to have to ask you, please, drink it out of your teacup."

The three of us fill our teacups and the stuff looks like water. Em says, "Well, here's mud in your eye!" I gulp some down. Boy! It's down there and it hits the chicken and the yams and all the fixings, and it hits the sherry. *Boom*! Em says, "How about another one?" Already one of Clarence's suspenders has slipped off. We sit there for fifteen minutes and Emily slips under the table.

Clarence stands up and says, "Get up off the floor, Em, you slob. Get up!" She gets up and her stockings are falling down.

He says, "Come on, we're going to go for a walk. Let's leave the young people together, heh?" And with that, Clarabelle comes into the dining room. Unbelievable! She makes Daisy Mae look like a Brownie.

Clarence says, "All right there. Remember, it's the USO, and anything for the boys!" And out go Clarence and Emily. From that moment on I've always loved the USO.

SHIPPING OUT

I'm in this camp in Missouri, in the foothills of the Ozarks, and it's bad news, I want to tell you, bad news. And, of course, you just sort of accept it—after a while you kind of get used to it. I'm going through all the obstacle courses, and I'm doing all this stuff, and the camp, if you'll excuse the expression, is hell on wheels. It is a bad-news camp. It would alternately rain, really rain, and then it would snow. Oh boy, would it snow! But it is never in between except at one point it would do neither of these—that's when it drops to thirty below zero. So it is up and down and back and forth and I am out in the pole-line yard, climbing up and down telephone poles. The temperature is about fifteen degrees and the sleet is coming down out of the Ozark hills. You learn a little about reality, with your climbers on and carrying that crosspiece up there and the wind is screaming, and down below me is this sergeant hollering and we're trying to get the wire up and break the record of Company L or some crazy thing like that. It is just like having a gigantic toothache twenty-four hours a day.

One day we come back into the mess hall and we sit glumly, and the word gets out that we are going to get shipped. None of us knows where we would be going but we are going to get shipped. I'm in this little band of malcontents, this Company K, and we are about to embark on our great career. Great career?—we're about to embark.

So day after day after day after day this goes. It seems to go on endlessly. If we aren't crawling through concrete culverts on our behinds, dragging our rifles, with the wind coming down our necks, through the mud and the slush, we are pretending we are out on the range and we are dry-firing our pieces. It goes on and on and on and on. It just gets to be one long kind of farrago, one long dance. And every morning the rain is beating down on the barracks and it's four thirty-five, and you hear the rain pouring down and the whistles blow and you wake up and you still taste last night's chow—salt pork and beans. The rain is dripping through the barracks and you can smell your fatigues, which have not been to the laundry for four weeks and they're gamey and you wake up and this yellow lightbulb is hanging over your head and this corporal from Tennessee is running around, "Okay, you guys, come on, you guys, put on them socks and let's get moving, let's go!"

Well, this goes on and on, and after what seems like a year of this, the word is out—all of a sudden it's announced that we are about to ship, that we are redlined, and we are going to leave on Friday. Boy, the excitement! Getting out of this to anyplace! We don't care where they send us. Send us to Hell, we don't care. Just get us out of this place. We'd had it up to here. Everybody's running around, all excited and we're getting our equipment all checked.

What do you think happens? The day before we are to ship I wake up and I am so sick, I can't believe it. Am I sick! I wake up and I don't know what it is. I am so weak, I'm shaking, just shaking and sweating. You don't sweat here, it's always cold here. And I have a headache, I feel rotten and I'm scared—I'm sick! I'm really sick, I feel chills, and really hot and then chills. So I get up and I fall out in the company street in the rain and the first sergeant is walking back and forth in front of the company and he is barking out orders. He's saying, "Well, mens, now, all you guys know that from now on we're under tight security. We are now alerted for shipment. We will have no letters home of rumors out as to where we are going 'cause the CO and I don't even know. The secret orders is sealed at battalion headquarters, and you guys know we are a high security radar outfit. We will have no talk. And any of you mens what needs any special medical treatment or anything like that, you will report down to the day room before we ship. Any questions?"

And I'm shaking and I'm so sick I can hardly stand up. One of the few times in my life that I've been so sick that I am swaying. I can't even hear what he is saying. I can just hear a ringing in my ears and my head hurts and up above my eyes I can feel a terrible pain just rocking through my head and at the same time my throat is so sore I can hardly talk, even to myself. Most of all, tremendous chills that last about a minute, and then enormous heat. Through the whole day we are out climbing poles, doing crazy things, and the whole day goes by like a fantastic nightmare, and the one thing over and over I keep saying to myself, "Don't let them find out. If they find out, you're sunk! The company's gonna ship and you're gonna be stuck here. And God knows where you'll be sent. Who knows—they may even keep you here in this hole."

I am afraid of going to the clinic because I know what would happen. They'd send me to the hospital right now and the company would ship and I am scared, really scared and everything is swirling. I can't even see. Finally the day is over and I don't even go to chow.

I sit on the edge of my bunk and I say to Gasser, "I'm really sick, man."

He says, "You better go down to the clinic, you don't know what you got. You may have spinal meningitis or something terrible."

I say, "I don't know. I can't do anything. If I go down there, man, I'm sunk."

I keep throwing up, I keep running down to the latrine. I'm afraid people will see me. The night goes by and I can't sleep, I'm just tossing and turning, and every five minutes I get up and run down to the latrine, and I am getting worse.

Finally, it's dawn. This is the day we are to ship. I get up and we are lined up in the company street with all of our equipment. Full pack, barracks bag, raincoat, helmet liner, M1—everything. We are ready, man. The rain is coming down. The first sergeant is calling the roll and the captain's all dressed up and the second lieutenants and a couple of staff sergeants all in their traveling Class A uniforms, and there's a train pulled up down at the end by Second Army headquarters.

Ten minutes later we march down by the train and they are checking off names and I can't even walk now and I say to Gasser, "You better hold me up, man, I'm going to pass right out." Well, we fake it. I get on the train and the train starts to roll. In a half hour we are at a siding and I know we're gone from camp and they can't do *anything* and I can let myself get sick. I just sort of let it go, I'm just sick.

The first sergeant comes back and says, "What's the matter with you?"

I say, "I'm sick."

"Why didn't you tell me? You mean to tell me you're gonna get sick on the train? Oh no! No!"

I say, "Yeah, I'm sick."

And then he says the only thing he ever said that was good to me. "I don't blame ya. I wouldn't have gone and stayed in that hole ever myself. Come on, come on." He grabs ahold of my neck and he drags me down to the end of the car where the medical officer is, who takes one look at me and says, "Make up his bunk."

They put me in one of these bunks. I wake up and I go swooning back to sleep. I'm out of my head all the time. Completely. And one of the guys brings me a mess kit once in a while and I say, "Oh, take it away, *oh, ahhh.*"

It just goes on and on like one long nightmare. I hear rattling and banging and crashing and I hear guys talking and once in a while I hear the sound of somebody hollering and I hear a card game going on and I sleep again, wake up, and my entire bunk is just bathed in sweat. I am delirious for a while. It is the worst journey I've ever made in my life.

Then I look out the window and I begin to notice things around me—I am getting better! I notice a little plaque above me and I keep looking at it and it says SEABOARD LINE. It is a car they got from that company. The name sticks in my mind. We are sixty-three hours on the rails, and I drift off again and then I wake up, and finally, at long last, we get to where we are going.

And the doors open and it is like a miracle cure. I don't know what I had. I get out of the train and I feel fifty pounds lighter. My uniform is falling off of me. The temperature is eighty degrees. I look back and see this big line of letters in gold leaf on the side of the train: SEABOARD LINE. And every time I see that name, Seaboard Line, I have this emotional thing. I feel my throat tightening up. The fear that I'm going to be redlined.

PART THREE

WARTIME
IN FLORIDA
IS
HELL

Many of Shepherd's Signal Corps stories take place in a semitropical, rather hellish environment. At Camp Murphy, just west of West Palm Beach, U.S. planes flew overhead to give the radar units practice tracking them. Sometimes he speaks of the early type of radar unit his company worked with as an SCR-268, an ungainly, rectangular piece of equipment, so heavy it required several strong trucks called "prime movers" to transport it. Later, dish antennas mercifully came into use.

Then there's the "poles"—essentially working as a circus acrobat high atop five-story-tall telephone poles. This training so scared Shep that he took the only way out—applying to radar maintenance and construction installation school. Hard to get into but not as hard as plummeting ninety feet to the ground when your "climbers" cut out.

Shepherd spent many interesting—but not especially happy— times in Florida, and some of the memories he brought back might be unpleasant, but he learned a lot.

The first story is about how Shepherd got his MOS—his Military Occupation Specialty—as a radar technician. The route to radar heaven began back in Camp Crowder's forest of pole line construction. A bleak field of poles.   —EB

MOS: RADAR TECHNICIAN

There was a great crowd of us in the great forest of denuded poles that looked like a forest that had been hit by some strange breed of locusts that ate all the branches off. There were a hundred poles—maybe a thousand in this bleak field, with the wind sweeping down out of the Ozarks.

Poor old Nash was hanging on the pole next to me and the wind was howling. Now I'm telling all this to demonstrate to you why I signed up for this school. You can understand the moment of desperation. But at this time I was hanging on. The wind was screaming by. Suddenly, I heard Nash—*AAAAAAAAAAAAAAAAAAA*! And I saw him swirl around and his climbers had cut out—that's a phrase they use—when your climbers cut out that means the spikes on your climbing shoes no longer are supporting you and you're about to descend rapidly. His climbers had cut out, and Nash did the worst thing you could do!

We had been instructed for weeks that if your climbers ever cut out, you only do one thing—you push away. You do not grab that pole. You push away and just trust to luck. There's a very good reason for this. Because you're on a pole that's made out of wood and you're up at the top and if the climbers cut out like that, you're going to descend. That belt that you've got around you is not a safety belt, it's a work belt. That's not there to keep you from harm. That belt is so, when you get up to the top of the pole, you can snap your belt on and you lean back and it works.

Well, the minute your climbers cut out, that belt is going to do nothing but keep you next to the pole, it's not going to keep you from falling. What happens if you fall right down a pole? Well, I'll tell you what happens, friend. I have known guys in the Signal Corps who climbed poles who had been gutted from one end to the other with slivers as long as fifteen feet. Yes, it's an awful thought, isn't it?

That was drummed into us hour after hour. What did Nash do? I heard him—*AAAAAAAAAAAAAAAAAAA*! I looked and I saw Nash's legs out at right angles from the pole. Obviously his climbers were not in the pole. I saw those two spikes sticking out—about three or four inches long and Nash was hanging by his arms at the top of the pole and he was slowly sliding down. As he slowly slid down, you heard him yelling and hollering, and the sergeant below hollered, "All right, Nash, push away. Push away, Nash!"

Well Nash wasn't gonna push away. He wasn't gonna do that, so he was hanging on the pole and as he slowly slid down, the sergeant, with his climbers on, went running up the pole like a monkey. And he got Nash by the foot. He was holding him up.

There was a moment when the entire company of pole line construction climbers suffered a complete company panic. Not one guy, but all of us. Everybody saw Nash hanging like that. Well, I said, the hell with this! I started to climb down.

The whole company in a panic was falling like leaves off their poles. Five feet from the safety of the ground, I fell and landed on my gas mask, and one foot climber's spike punctured my boot all the way through the sole. I heard guys yelling and hollering and hitting the ground.

And I made up my mind, this is not for me. This ain't my dish of tea, to put it mildly. When the wounded had been picked up and the disaster had been cleared off, and I was sitting back in the day room at night, I thought, "I've got to get out of this! Ain't no way of getting out!" You're in this thing, see. You just couldn't go down to the orderly room and say, "Sergeant, I've been thinking it over. I quit. This is ridiculous. I quit this stuff." It just doesn't work like that. But there are ways to do it.

Thirty-nine guys and myself sat in an army theater when we received our MOS. We were graduating from the school of radar maintenance ultra-high-frequency school techniques. I'll never forget sitting there in that crowd and hearing that major say things like, "Well, we'd like to congratulate all of you. There's no telling where you're going to go now, no telling what's going to happen, but you're all expert radar men now."

RADAR AT FIFTEEN THOUSAND VOLTS

I'm in this radar company, Company K, and we were deep in the heart of the jungle. And it was hot. Oh, my God Almighty it was hot. The temperature about one hundred and five degrees all the time. Terrible. Not only hot all the time but the humidity was four hundred percent. You can't believe the air can have so much water in it. You could cause rainstorms by clapping. And heat rash.

But that wasn't what bothered us. You can get used to weather. You know what bothered us? Our radar set. We had a radar set that had fifteen thousand volts on the plate. Back in the days when they had electric chairs, they operated at one thousand eight hundred to two thousand volts. So you can figure out what fifteen thousand volts are. At one-point-five amps. That is powerful stuff. Roughly enough power to blow up the city of Trenton, just like that.

Our power supply came in a big package about the size of a ten-by-twelve room, by seven feet high, and it operated on trucks that had great big sets of wheels under them that were called prime movers. Tremendous power supply. And it had a great big wheel on it that was called a Variac. When you turned that thing up it increased the power on our radar equipment. When this thing was fully fired up, this piece of radar gear stood something like sixty feet in the air. Big baby! Oh, we were so scared of that thing.

There were rumors floating around about what it had done to guys. One of the most evil rumors came around when I was sitting up there on the azimuth-scope one day, got a pair of earphones on my head, and I was looking into that scope. One of the guys said into the cans, "Hey, did you hear what this stuff does to ya?"

I said, "What? What stuff?"

"It's the radiation coming out of this thing."

"What?"

"It makes you sterile."

Whap! It hit the entire company—our radar was not only taking our life, squeezing our veins, sucking our juice out of us—on top of it, it was making us sterile! So we'd make a wide circle around that radar set. It was the enemy.

It went twenty-four hours a day. Twenty-four hours a day. We had this generator set back in the vines there. It was called a Leroy engine. It went *chutchutchutchutchutchutchutchutchutchutch utchut.* You'd listen to that twenty-four hours a day, man, and your head was popping! You just sort of jiggled to that beat. You'd lie in your bunk and it'd go *chutchutchutchutchutchutchutchut.* Try that on for size for a year and a half, and you'll know that your head has turned to jelly. Well, it was popping away there. The biggest fear we had, though, was of those fifteen thousand volts.

There were rumors that in one company, three GIs were working on the power supply and it had been turned off for over three weeks. It just had the power it retained in the condensers— BOOOOM! Ionized! Three GIs. Nothing found of them! Just *pow!* Ionized! Three GIs turned into a purple haze, and they just blew away when the wind came. Well, we were scared.

And every couple of days we'd have to turn this thing down and check the tubes and all that jazz. That was when it scared us the most. Because then you'd have to start messing with the controls! One day we were down for repairs. We'd been tuning the antennas, we'd been working on the power supply, doing things with the azimuth-scope.

Lieutenant Cherry comes out of his tent and says, "All right. Okay, you guys over there at the power supply. Turn on the filaments. I want to see the filaments on the sixteen-hundreds now, let's go. *Gunkgunkgunk*! Guys are throwing relays and every time they throw a relay they start moving back. *Gunkgunkgunk*. Red light. Blue lights. *Gunkgunkgunk*. Now the filaments are on.

Two minutes go by and the big green light comes on, and that means the tubes are warmed up and it's ready to go. With that, Lieutenant Cherry says. "All right, turn it up to two kilovolts. Two kilovolts. Give me two KV on the plate." So poor old Ernie grabs that big wheel and he turns it up, and the meter goes up to two kilovolts. Whenever we started to turn up that fifteen-thousand-volt plate, guys would start backing away, because for a year and a half we always expected that thing to blow up. You know how it is, you expect disaster all your life and you're never really ready for it when it hits. So Ernie turns it up to two kilovolts and Lieutenant Cherry says, "Everything reading okay up there, you guys on the top? Everything all right?"

"Yo, yo." You know how it is, you holler "Yo, yo."

Cherry says, "Turn it up to three kilovolts. Everything reading okay up there?"

"Yo." "Yo." "Yo." "Yo." Everyone's reading his meter.

"All right, turn it up to four kilovolts, move it up, let's go." So Ernie turns it up to four kilovolts.

All of a sudden, out of the top of that power supply pack there's a thin wisp of blue smoke! It's coming out! And a sound is going *Shiiiiiiiiiiiiiiiiiiiiiiiiiiiiii*. Every GI dives for the ground. We'd built these beautiful slit trenches that nobody ever used, and all of us dive into them and the big power supply is going *shiiiiiiiiiiiiashiiiiiiiiiiiashiiiiiiiiii*. Blue smoke pouring out. Blue smoke trailing to the skies. Guys lying there, figuring it's all over, it's going to blow. It goes *kapooo*—with a little pop.

Then a siren sound, *wooooooooooooooooaaaaa woooaaaaaaaa*. We all lie there and wait. Then we realize. Somebody had stuck one of those fake bombs in this thing, the kind they put in cars that say, TURN ON THE IGNITION, SURPRISE YOUR FRIENDS! They make a whistling sound and blow up and make smoke and are responsible for a lot of unexpected laundry bills.

We just lie there and Lieutenant Cherry comes up out of his hole with his GI helmet on and he says, "All right! I'm gonna find out who put that damn bomb in that power supply or I'm gonna bust every stripe in this outfit. Any of you know who done it? I'm gonna bust you right down to buck-ass privates. All of you get outta them holes and we're gonna start an investigation."

We never did find out who did it. All I know is, from then on, nobody really took radar seriously. It was just sort of a big Tinkertoy.

SWAMP RADAR

We were assigned to the 3162nd Signal Air Warning Radar Unit, which at one point was posted deep into the heart of the Florida Everglades, and we were putting together our little unit for the trip down there. We had three little jeeps, our troop carrier, and two "prime movers," which were rotten trucks with bad valves and bad carburetors. Gigantic trucks, and on the back of each was an enormous cabinet filled with our hard-hitting U.S. Signal Corps efficient equipment, consisting of a radar unit that had been sent over to us by the British, with all British markings and screws that went backwards. Terrible stuff.

We drove deeper and deeper into the swamp. It got hotter and hotter as we went. Up front sitting there in the forward jeep was our poor, sad, pock-marked captain, who used to teach English at Northwestern, who had dreams of being on General Eisenhower's staff and making command decisions. And there he was heading deeper and deeper into the muck with a bunch of nearsighted T5s and a secondhand radar unit. Finally we got to this tiny town—there really are people living in the Everglades in places you couldn't conceive of. Nothing but water and heavy moss and the smell of millions of dead lizards that had died over the last ten million years. And there they sat—the Florida crackers. Our little unit arrived at that town and we had to go ten miles further.

After three months in our final location our unit had begun to fit in and we had begun to accept things. We wore nothing but torn shorts. Each one of us was one big mosquito bite, a big pimple with feet. And all of us with a strange, green-yellow fungus that covered us like moss. We looked like the rocks and the trees. We'd scratch and put a thick butter of sulfa salve on us. We'd leave trails of grease and glop. There were thirty-eight of us. Oh, boy, you learned about mankind when you lived with thirty-eight guys in a steaming jungle for a while. You learned every possible crotchet, every possible hang-up, and new hang-ups all of a sudden broke out. You just had to accept them. Guy sitting there and he'd been eating a Dashiell Hammett book—just eating it. He really dug mysteries—okay, accepted! You got so you'd accept things.

We'd arrived down there in February or March, three months had passed, and every succeeding day was hotter by a tenth of a degree than the day before. Eerie. We had this equipment so we had to keep a temperature check, and it just kept going up and up. Ninety-nine point eight, you'd check it off. Next day ninety-nine point nine. The humidity was one-oh-five and your ears were steaming. Always. If you moved your hand quickly, it rained. You had the sense of constantly just swimming under water. Hot water. Swim and swim and every day it got hotter.

Now how did we live? This is the kind of stuff no war books ever tell you about. We were living in what they call pyramidal tents. A pyramid with sides, and there were six guys in each tent, one bunk on each side and two in the middle. Made of this peculiar waterproof material that just kept the water in. Catch it all during the day, and you'd go to the "tank" that night to sleep. You'd lie there and you'd smell. Smells are very important to us as animals. Smells are constantly with us, and whenever I think of the army I think of that peculiar smell of the waterproof canvas tent. Sort of like old gasoline, a little touch of tar, and a kind of overtone of Smith Brothers cough drops. And with that, the smell of fatigues from last month piled up in the corner.

Then, the great historic moment when I got into town. Every three days one of us would be allowed to go into the little town and stand and, for a while, watch the pool room—which was off limits. One of the natives said to me, "Yeah, you know you gotta get used to this place, I guess. 'Course you're lucky you ain't here in the mosquito season." And there I was, wearing my mosquito net and drinking Flit. I said, "I'm not in the mosquito season!?"

I got back to our unit and I sat in our tent and I could hear nothing but this humming all around. It was a hundred and five degrees and Gasser came in. For the last month Gasser had been reduced to just wearing his Johnson and Johnson athletic supporter. That's all he was wearing. He came in out of the mosquitoes and I said, "Gasser, one of the boys in front of the pool room just told me we're here in the good season."

Gasser was scratching. He said, "What?"

I said, "Well, you see, it ain't mosquito season yet, Gasser."

We had been under the sun for about four months and we were the color of old leather, and Gasser just paled a little bit. He said, "Not mosquito season?"

I said, "No, Gasser."

And all the while, all around us as we sat there and talked—no, it wasn't the hum—you got so used to the hum that you didn't hear it anymore. Like living in New York and you don't hear the traffic anymore. But sometimes I wake up in New York at two o'clock in the morning even now and in my dream I'd been hearing those sounds of living in the Everglades. We had to generate our own power and we had a maniacal little insane device known as a "Leroy Engine and Generator M2." The Leroy engine went *dutdutdutdutdutdutdutdutdutdut* night and day, twenty-four hours a day, seven days a week, thirty-one days a month, three hundred sixty-nine million days a year. You just sat there and it went *dutdutdutdutdutdutdutdutdut* and you got to the point where you just sort of talked real loud. This insane *tom tom* hour after hour and whining its way through it was this sound of the radar keying unit. A 440-cycle note. Roughly an A note. Can you imagine a pitch pipe blowing at you for all of your life in one hundred and five degrees, with mosquitoes chiming *eeeeeeeeeeeeeeeee*, our radar unit down there keying *eeeeeeeeeeeeeeeeeeeeeeeeee* and *dutdutdutdutdutdutdutdut* and once in a while you'd hear the muffled scream of a GI in the distance.

And time began to have absolutely no meaning, because our radar unit worked twenty-four hours a day. You didn't know when you were going to be on and so they'd wake you up, you'd be lying there in your pool of sweat. You'd be amazed how you could sweat so much. You couldn't believe you could sweat anymore and you'd sweat four more quarts. A guy flashed a light in your eyes and you didn't even say anything, you just got up. *Dutdutdutdutdutdutdutdut eeeeeeeeeeeeeee!*

You go out there and there is that *insane* radar unit. You hate it like Ahab hates Moby Dick. It's up there, very big, and it just keeps going around, those great big dipole antennas looking down on those palm trees, and you hear the wind blowing through them. We always understand that wind is a romantic idea to us in the woods, wind blowing through the spruce trees—*ooooooh*, but I got so I couldn't stand the sound of the wind. It's blowing through this idiotic, insane radar unit. It goes *ohhhhhhhhhhhhhhhhhhhhhhh* and then it gets slightly to the windward and it gets out of the wind, *wohhhh*. You're sitting there waiting for it to go again, and then it goes around *wohhhhhhhhhhh*, and all the while the keying unit is going *eeeeeeeeeeeeeeeeeeeeeeeeeee*. And playing around the tops of this insane, maniacal nut is St. Elmo's Fire.

Three nights out of eight we have all the proper magical qualities in nature put together—St. Elmo's Fire, a kind of static electricity only rotten, a whole bunch of little blue-green ghosts just running back and forth on the dipoles, back and forth, and you sit there for the next four hours, your sweat pouring down and you have a hood over your eyes, and you're watching that PPI, that little scope, that little line going *wrnggg wrnggg wrnggg* and it just keeps going round and round and round, just round and round and you sit, you get hotter, and after a while you get completely—and I don't think this has ever been recorded—you lose complete consciousness of yourself, you're an abstract mind, you don't feel your body, you don't know what time it is, there's no such thing as day, it must be the way it'll be with space travelers, there's no day, there's no night, there's no summer, there's no winter, there's no other people even.

Once in a while you pull out, away from that PPI, and you look down and there you see, about fifteen feet away in the darkness, this other, huddled figure. And when you're out there in the darkness and you get to windward, you smell 'im. And you get so you know the smell of all the guys—you know Gasser, you know Dunker, you know them all. You don't have to say, "Hey, Gasser," you just say something. We're just sitting there. And it's going round and round and round and every night, what do you think we're looking for? German submarines.

German submarines. Once every three or four nights you're staring, looking for a little pip on the screen, and this is what made it such an eerie experience. I don't know any experience in civilian life like it. You're quietly surveying the great ocean out there lying off the East Coast of Florida. Just see those PPI lines. You've got a pair of cans, and once in a while you hear somewhere off in the distance the OP. You hear whoever is the officer on duty say, "Hey,

Gasser, the coffee hot?" And somebody shoves a cup of coffee in your hand. You don't even know it, you just get this big mug of this hotter-than-the-outside-air, that's all it is. Drink a little of it while waiting for a submarine.

Weeeeeeee, and suddenly, without any warning, there's a dot! You can't believe it. You stop and say, "Hey, P forty degrees hold it. Sweep seven degrees left, seven degrees right," *weeeee* and it goes *weeeee*. By god, there's a pip! There's something out there! Somehow you welcome those Germans. Hello, guys. They've been under water for four years. And a funny part of it is, you know what they would do, they would come up to the surface to hang out their wash. You don't hear about those things. They'd come up to the surface to recharge their batteries and hang out their wash. Here's our radar unit, it goes *weeeeee*! And it sort of hovers. Everything stops. You don't hear the sound of the *pocketa pocketa* engine. You forget the mosquitoes, you forget it all. You've got that little, tiny pip. That little thing keeps sweeping *weeeeeeeeeeee weeeeeeeeeeeeeee*. And there it is. The first feeling you have is, Oh, god, am I going to make an idiot of myself? You don't want to tell somebody that it's there. You can't believe it at first. But it's there, it's there! There's three of us on these little seats in the darkness. Absolutely removed from everyone else. And I say, "Hey, Gasser, do you see it?"

Gasser says, "Yeah."

"Dunker, you see it?"

"Yeah. Let's take another sweep. Maybe it'll go away."

Se we go *weeeeeeeeeeeeeeeeeeeeeeee*. Nothing. We pick up Miami. *Weeeeeeeeeeeeeeeeeee. Goingggggggggggg*! He's there! He's there!

And then, invariably Dunker says, "Hey, Gasser, will you get the repair NCO?" We don't believe our radar unit is working. We never believed it. Get the repair NCO.

So we crank the radio and five minutes later this master sergeant arrives. "Whatsa matter? Lemme see." *Weeeeeeeeeeeeeeee.* He says, "It's a pip. Get the second lieutenant. Something's wrong with the set."

Nobody believes anything in the army. After about forty minutes of this it is finally decided that there is something out there. All the while we've got listening devices that are trying to pick up the surface sounds. We've got radios, DF equipment trying to pick him up. And they finally have located this little German sub, lying on the surface there and you can hear the guys talking about the automatic washer. "Bring me some more soap, Fritz." You hear them talking.

Somebody says, "Red alert. Give the red alert!" The red alert in the middle of the jungle! It's blackness! There's nobody there! Red alert? The army loves words like that. It makes them feel like "Operation Blitz!" Four little guys like Rip Torn charge! Operation Blitz! Red alert!

So we send a radio message to the nearest town, which is on Jupiter Island, and it's sent back to another place and another place and we sit and watch, waiting for our peerless armed forces to take care of the sub. We're just watching. These are scenes you never read about in war books. True? We just watch that sub, see.

I'll never forget this night. We're sitting there watching this sub, the three of us watching the scope. At the center of the scope is the pivot point of the line that sweeps around *whoooooooooooooooo,* and anything out there is a little dot that the sweeping line picks up. The sub is lying right there. It's just a little dot on the scope, you know. You gaze at a scope for four years, boy, and some guys are still hypnotized by it. Their wives wonder why they get that funny look in the eyes *whooooooooooooooooo.* Every time they look at their TV set *whooooooooooooooooo,* they see the coast of Tripoli go past. And this night we're sitting there—these are unrecorded moments in the war and we're watching a sub that's lying about a mile off the coast.

We hadn't believed it but it was obviously a pip that had not been there. It's there now as the three of us watch at four o'clock in the morning. We're watching this insane little thing. And we had the feeling that we were really looking at Germany. This is it, a little dot right here. You know it's peculiar when you can reduce a whole nation, an entire ideology, the enemy—to a tiny pinpoint of light. A fantastic concept of war.

We are watching. A half hour goes by. Nothing happens. We have alerted the entire coast. The navy is supposed to be sending planes. Nothing. And then, all of a sudden, in the upper right hand corner of our scope is another pinpoint of light. And it's going directly toward the first one.

And Gasser says, "What's that?"

Dunker says, "It's a freighter. It's a freighter!"

I say, "Wait, let's sweep back again." *Wheeeeeeeee.* By god, it is! Another ship is out there in the darkness and it's getting closer to the first one that's lying on the surface.

Gasser picks up the phone. He starts the call—*engrrr engrrr*—like that. "A pip at quadrant three. Proceeding about six knots, yeah. A mile and an eighth offshore, yeah. I don't know! *That's not my problem!*"

It's getting closer and closer. Nothing is happening. No airplanes. Not a sound except the sound of the mosquitoes and the sound of that insane motor, *dutdutdutdutdutdutdutdutdut.* And we're watching the entire war.

That little dot gets closer and closer. Gasser keeps calling up. And then those two dots are so close together they begin to merge.

And then *boooooom*! We hear a funny sound. Have you ever heard a real explosion? You don't really hear it, it just sort of hits you. It just goes *blump*! And we pull back from the scope and we see, way out in the darkness, a great red cloud going higher and higher. Way up in the air. We're just watching.

And now there is only one pip. Just one, and it's lying there. They've surfaced again and they're moving a little off to the right to see how they did. We see this great red glow in the sky. They had hit a high octane aviation gasoline transport. She has gone up like one big firecracker.

We watch that pip for about fifteen minutes, with the mosquitoes getting more and more aggressive and then we hear the sound of an airplane. One hour and ten minutes has passed since our first alert and we hear, coming down from the left, somewhere up in the north end of Florida, we hear *dupdupddupdupdupdup*. It is a Piper Cub.

It's a Piper Cub. We pick him up on the scope and Dunker says, "What the devil is that?! Is *that* the Navy? It's hardly moving!"

We look up and there's this little Piper CAP plane. It's being flown by a dentist on his day off from Jacksonville. He has been alerted to look at what those nutty Signal Corps guys are up to again! He flies out and he takes one look at that sub and they look up at him and they unlimber their 20mm cannon and just go *bumbumbumbum*. He turns around and comes tearing back and sweeps about ten feet over our heads. He is on his way now to Cleveland. He doesn't want anything to do with this.

A little while later the pip disappeared. That was it. That was an incident in the war. That was one battle. A hundred and eighty-two guys went up on the ship. Later that morning we saw that ship, just the mast sticking up out of the water and the whole shoreline covered with pieces of rubble and empty life rafts.

NIGHT MANEUVERS

I'm out on a night maneuver and our entire company is down in the swamps of the Everglades. In fact, there are about twenty-five companies on a vast night field maneuver that is to take place. Do you know what really happens on a night maneuver when soldiers get out there in the dark? Nothing. Everything goes to pieces. Individual guys have no idea what's happening. There's a peculiar chaotic quality that happens when this *thing* gets under way.

We're all standing in the dark there one night, we're all wearing our tropical gear, and our mosquito netting, and insect repellant rubbed all over our faces. Preparing for swamp warfare. Oh, boy! I don't think there's any place scarier than a swamp. You spend a night in a swamp, and man, you just don't forget it! I'll never forget it for the rest of my born days.

Me and Goldberg are assigned to a twisted pair of telephone lines we are supposed to string over to Company C's command post. We all stand, waiting to be loaded on the trucks. Each one has been assigned his task. Each guy knows exactly what he has to do. I have a big reel of wire attached to my pack on my back. Goldberg has a field telephone set attached to him, and the two of us are a "wire-lane, company-observation-post team." Me and Goldberg.

You've seen these movies of Van Johnson, he's lying in a hole and he's a captain, he's the commanding officer, and he's got his telephone that he keeps cranking. And he says, "Charlie Company here calling battalion headquarters. Charlie Company here." *Poom!*

Poom! The mortars are going overhead. That is what they call a command post field telephone, strung by wires back to the command post. His boss, the major, is about two hundred yards back in the darkness, hiding in his hole, which is a little larger. That's the command post. And he's got about three of these wires coming in. Each guy cranks when he wants to talk to him.

Goldberg and I are to lay one of these twisted pairs of wires, from our company to battalion headquarters, which is maybe two hundred yards away. And our company takes off into the dark. *Tramp, tramp, tramp, tramp.* And the mosquitoes start to move in and the heat is coming up from the swamp. You can smell the dead toads. You smell that brackish, salty kind of water that's in swamps. You can smell the mud. The smell of mud is a very distinctive smell. And guys in New York, we're so removed from nature—this must have been one of the smells that the dinosaurs smelled. Mud is mud. It must have been exactly the kind of smell that the earliest primitive man smelled as he crawled out of those ancient swamps. That smell of mud gets stronger and stronger and richer and riper and deeper and rounder as you go further and further into the swamps.

And we're following the trail that has been supposedly laid down for us by the advanced scouts of our signal battalion. It gets so dark, so black, so many mosquitoes, that we gradually begin to lose track of one another, until finally there's just two of us left. So help me. Me and Goldberg. We can hear the others rattling around in the darkness. We can hear an occasional muffled curse. We can hear somewhere the sound of a truck slowly pulling out of mud and it is all getting further away until finally there's me and Goldberg hiding in a hole next to a great big cliff that runs up and over to a clump of trees and down again into some more water.

I whisper, "Hey, Goldberg. Goldberg."

He whispers, "Yeah, what're we gonna do?"

"I don't know. Let's wait. Somebody's gonna come along."

He whispers, "Yeah."

And off in the distance you hear another muffled curse. Little do we realize that what we're hearing is two other guys in another hole—lost.

"Hey, Goldberg, I'll go out and see if I can find the command post. You stay here."

"Don't go! Don't go!"

"What do you mean? Why not?"

"I'm scared."

"So am I. You come with me."

So the two of us crawl over the top of the cliff. We are crawling through kind of a path, but not really. It's a small space between two beds of quicksand. We're crawling along and I've got my wire behind me.

I say, "Gasser, hey, Gasser!" Gasser was in the other team. "Hey, Gasser!"

I hear somewhere off in the distance, "What do ya want?"

I say, "Hey, Gasser, where's the CP?"

"How the hell should I know?"

"What are we gonna do, Gasser?"

He says, "I don't know."

Long, pregnant pause. We crawl another thirty feet and high overhead, something arches into the sky and it goes *poooohh*! It's a star shell. We're supposed to watch for a red starshell and if one goes off, that means we're under attack! That little red thing hangs there like a ball from a roman candle—just puffs like that. It floats a little bit. Gasser says, "Hey, they're after us!" and Goldberg says, "Lay down!"

We lie there for about, I'd say, six weeks, in the darkness. And about thirty feet away something starts to flash in the water. And it is no person. It keeps going *hauuuup! hauuuup! hauuuup! hauuuup! hauuuup!* Goldberg says, "What's that?" "I don't know." *hauuuup! hauuuup!* About four hundred yards away, I hear Gasser say, "Is that you, Shepherd? What are you doing?" "Nothing. I'm lying here. Shut up!"

Poooohh! Another star shell goes up *poooohh!* It drifts overhead. And now we're starting to get scared. I mean really scared. What happens if the company commander discovers that nothing's working? We got no phones—nothing. We've been training for this thing for about a month. And now we're lying in a hole.

Hauuuup! hauuuup! That thing starts to grunt again. *Hauuuup! hauuuup!* And then I hear something slither right next to me *pshoooo shoooo.* "Hey, Goldberg, is that you?" "No, what was it?" I say, "It sounded like a snake."

He says, "A *what*?" Goldberg was the most citified guy I ever knew. His dad owned a delicatessen over on the West Side, and the sneakiest thing he had ever seen is the time that a salami got away off the truck. So now he is petrified and we're both lying there in the dark. Nobody, in our orders, nobody once in all our training, had discussed what happens in the dark if you run into a snake. What do you do in the dark if you run into an alligator?

And, by George, just about this time, the alligator opens up. Have you ever heard an alligator—in the dark? The alligator's mating cry goes a little bit like this—he goes *mraaah, mraaah, mraaaaaaahhhghaaaa. Mraaah.* And he lies there for a minute waiting to see if anybody's taking a nibble. Then he flaps his tail a little in the mud, just a little bit. You can just hear the tail—*puck-puck.* He sounds like he's thirty feet long. We lie there in the dark. I've got the wire on my back, Goldberg has the field set on his back. Gasser's got his wire on his back and with him is Edwards, who has a field set, too. Nobody moves for about an hour.

Then there's a splash. You can hear the sound of that alligator swimming away, *phooo phooo, mraaa mraaa*. He's gone.

Another star shell goes up. This time it's a white one. The white one means all clear. We are no longer under attack. Move forward!

"So, where we gonna go, Goldberg? We're supposed to go somewhere."

He says, "I ain't goin' nowhere."

I say, "I ain't either. I ain't gonna get lost in that quicksand."

I hear a whisper maybe forty or fifty feet away. Then something crawls past me. Right past me. I can see it outlined against the sky. I can see a tin hat.

I say, "Where are you goin', mac?"

He says, "Don't bother me."

I say, "Where are you goin'?"

He says, "I'm looking for the command post."

I say, "So am I."

He says, "I don't know where it is. It was supposed to be over here."

I say, "No, it's supposed to be up over there."

He says, "Don't get in my way, I gotta go, cryin' out loud!"

I say, "Lemme go with you."

He says, "No, stay where you are."

He crawls about twenty feet and then turns around and comes back. He says, "Hey, you guys, mind if I hide here with you a couple of minutes?"

I say, "No."

He sneaks down into the hole. Now there's three of us sitting in it. And there's just the slight edge of dawn beginning to appear now over the eastern horizon way off in the distance. Another star shell goes up—*phet*! and arches down. And this third guy says, "Damnit!"

I say, "What's the matter?"

He says, "We gotta get goin'. We can't stay here."

I say, "Yeah, but where we gonna go?"

He says, "I don't know."

And then I begin to see on his helmet in the vague glint of dawn, a single white bar. It's a first lieutenant! He's one of our company officers! And Goldberg sees it at the same time. He puts his head down, just sits there with his feet up. I sit there looking out across the swamp.

This guy says, "Hey, you guys. Hey, what company you from?"

With my quick GI mind I say, "Company M."

He says, "M Company? I thought you guys were from K!"

I say, "No, we're from Company M."

He says, "Oh, cryin' out loud! I'm with the wrong company!" And over the hill he goes. He was our first lieutenant. He was even more lost than we were! We thought we were from M Company! We were actually from K Company!

We sat for another minute and a half and Goldberg says, "Wow! Man, that's using the noodle!"

"What was I gonna do?"

"I don't know."

Long, pregnant pause.

Goldberg says, "I think he was puttin' us on. I'll bet he knew who we were."

I say, "No. He was lost, too. What do you think he was doin' here?"

He says, "I don't know. I bet he was out looking for guys who are goofing off."

I say, "We're not goofing off. We can't find nothin'."

Then Gasser pipes up off in the distance, "Hey, you guys, who was that lieutenant who just went by?"

I say, "Keep your head down, Gasser."

And the dawn comes up, and somewhere, from off to the left, a truck rattles down between two small puddles and we can see where we are. A couple of palm trees, a little palmetto, Gasser lying on a sand dune with Edwards, and there are the long tracks of where the alligator had gone past us. He had left one swampy lowland and gone across a small sandy rise to another. And the sky is running over us and it looks so innocent, all of it.

We'd had no idea where we were. It had all gone to pieces. And it hit me—where was Gregory Peck? When he runs a company it never happens like this. I've never seen one movie where all the guys get lost and sit in their holes and wait. Not one movie!

And three hours later we are all lined up in front of our tents. And the CO, our captain, is walking up and down in front of us and he's saying, "Men, I want to tell you that this was one of the most successful night field maneuvers that I have ever been involved in. And I also want to say that we have received a commendation from the colonel. And I want to congratulate each and every one of you for doing your jobs well. Training pays off!" And he walks back to the orderly room.

Gasser and I go to our tent and sit down. My spool of wire is back on the truck. Goldberg's field telephone is back on the shelf, and not a single message had passed to company headquarters, to CP, to battalion, to anywhere. And that night I learn sompin' real big. That night I learn—don't try to figure out anything. Just go along. Hold on. Ad lib. Fake it. 'Cause everybody else is ad libbing. Everybody else is fakin' it. Lieutenants, colonels, generals, majors, corporals, Pfcs, senators, presidents, vice presidents, premiers, all of them. All of them trying to make out as best as they can. All hiding in holes, sending up flares once in a while and whispering, "Hey, is it okay over there?" "How's it going?" "What do you mean, you're lost?" "So am I." "We can't both be lost." "Somebody's gotta know where it is."

Yeah, waiting for Godot. Waiting for Gregory Peck. Waiting for Van Johnson to get on Company Charlie's phone to tell us that the attack is going forward, and everything is under control. And somewhere tonight, Goldberg is out there, sitting behind the counter of his dad's delicatessen. Goldberg, who never once took his field telephone off his back, and here sits Shepherd, who never unspooled an inch of his wire, and somewhere, way, way out there is Gasser, with his roll of wire, and Edwards, with his telephone, and our commanding officer—God only knows where he is. He never got the message through.

LISTER BAG ATTACK

It was Company K, the 362 Signal Air Warning Group, a fantastically boring outfit. It had a great name though, didn't it? The biggest thing that would happen was that every three or four weeks, some guy would get busted and that would keep us going for another three or four weeks. Or every six or seven months somebody would tear the felt on the pool table and a fistfight would break out and that would keep us going for a while.

One thing, throughout the boredom, was the constant sound of our Leroy engine—did I ever tell you about the guy who flipped his cork one time on the mess line? He really flipped his wig. You always hear about guys flipping their wig. And I was standing at the end of a mess line one day and it was hot. Oh, boy, it was a hundred and forty degrees down there in the tropics with nothing but little palmettos all around us, nothing but sand and little scrubby pine trees and it was a hundred and forty degrees and you could hear in the background the sound of that Leroy engine go *pudapudapudapuda pudapudapudapuda*.

Ohhhhhhahhh, if I ever hear another one of those four-cylinder generators! A Leroy engine is a singularly angry kind of a diesel engine that is nasty in a lot of ways. First of all, it stinks. Very stinky motor. It blows this stink out at you all the time—just *pudapudapudapuda pudapudapudapuda*—when it goes. When it doesn't go it's about as lively as a rock. You have to work on it. It's greasy and cruddy and crummy and heavy.

Pudapudapudapuda, we were standing in line one day, we'd been there for—oh—two hundred years, I'd say. There were a couple of guys in the line who were left over from the Boer War. We were all standing in line and you heard *pudapudapudapuda pudapudapudapuda*. How'd you like to have about nine years of your life accompanied with that? *Pudapudapudapuda*. That was a Leroy engine that was driving an SCR 271 radar set, *pudapudapudapuda*. We got so our whole life was based on that beat. So you were trying to write a letter and you had this little piece of paper, this crummy little awful paper that had little Signal Corps flags on it. Trying to write and it was going *pudapudapudapuda*, and you bounced up and down. Funny, your writing all came out like little scratches, like shorthand *pudapudapudapuda*. Guys would be polishing their shoes *pudapudapuda* with the same beat.

So it was just going along like that one day, about twelve-thirty in the afternoon, and we were all standing in the chow line when suddenly, all around us, millions—trillions—of tiny gnats that were so small that you couldn't even see them. They started stinging everybody. Then they went away *pudapudapudapuda*, it went like that.

And hanging over there from a palmetto tree was our Lister bag. A Lister bag is a curious device. It looks like the bottom side of a cow strung up with the tail side down, and that bottom has chromium udders on it, four of them. And they fill it with lukewarm water, which they immediately put seventeen pounds of powdered chlorine in, as well as two and a half pounds of iodine, seventeen pounds of potash, and there's another chemical, which I fail to remember at this point, but this is a chemical which is supposed to make you not want to look at pinups.

So this was hanging there, big cow's udder, and the heat was booming down on it, and a corporal came walking along and he had a little piece of ice about the size of a Ping-Pong ball. He walked along and everybody saw him with the ice, and he walked up to the Lister bag and he dropped the little Ping-Pong ball of ice into the top of the Lister bag, turned around and hollered, "Ice water for any of you guys that want it."

Ice water. That forty-two-gallon Lister bag had been hanging in the sun now since the last few days of the Spanish-American War. It had scum on it, nobody drank out of that crummy thing. And the guy standing directly ahead of me all of a sudden began to pace back and forth. It's not easy to pace back and forth in a mess line. He was pacing around, back and forth he was going. He paced back and forth, back and forth he went. Back and forth, and he looked me right in the eye, turned around and paced the other way, turned around and looked me right in the eye again and turned around. And all the while the gnats again *reeeeeeeeeee*! And that motor *pudapudapudapuda*, and we could smell the fried grease we were going to have for lunch. You could smell it drifting in a grayish-bluish smoke among the trees *pudapudapudapudapuda*.

The sun is hanging there, and all of a sudden this guy turns around, and without any warning at all, he pulls this knife out of his pocket. He has a knife! It's an entrenching tool—he looks at me. I say, "Uh-oh. He's flipped his wig!" He turns, he runs right over a hill, down a hill, right over another little hill, and he sticks this knife right in the Lister bag—*bahhhaaaaa blauhhhhg* and the water flies out. Two hundred ninety-seven guys from Company K, the 362 Signal Air Warning Group watch this green, smelly water with the potash and the peralmutter and the Lava soap, and what's left over from a few old bars of Ivory, and that little Ping-Pong ball of ice, and it rolls out onto the sand.

Then he comes back—and stands in the line. Well, you don't ask him, you know. It's just kind of a funny thing. It's pointless to ask, "Why did you stab the Lister bag?" He just sort of stands there for a minute, and along comes a staff sergeant, calm-looking, cool cat, walking along. He's got pressed fatigues. He taps this guy on the shoulder and says, "Hey, come on."

The guy looks at him.

"Come on, come on," the sergeant says, without raising his voice, "Come on, let's go, mac." And they walk over the hill and they walk over the next hill and they disappear in the direction of the post hospital.

And that's the last we ever saw of him. End the vignette. Can't you see Rip Torn playing that one? *The Case of the Punctured Lister Bag,* or, *The Camel That Broke the Ping-Pong Ball of Ice's Back*?

I think it was that piece of ice that did it. I think it was that final slap in the face. And ten minutes later we're all lined up, sitting there in the mess hall and we're enjoying a cup of that fantastic brew which I still miss—the Purple Death.

BOREDOM ERUPTS

The only fistfight that I ever saw—I'm talking about a real fistfight—not just guys pushing each other around or guys belting each other—happened in a tent. How many times have you seen fights in the army? How do they come about? In the movies, what do guys fight about in the army? Usually it's James Whitmore and he's about to fight with somebody like Rip Torn. And there's always the Southern sergeant played by Rod Steiger who says, "Ain't no Yankee gonna say that toward *nobody*!" This is what fights are always about—the movie version of life.

It was eight o'clock in the evening, and it was after chow. Boredom hung heavy over the company area. So heavy that you could just cut it with your trench knife if you wanted to. Make little balls out of it and toss them back and forth and play catch with them. And I came wandering down the company street little realizing that I was about to observe a scene. And, in fact, I would be part of the scene, which I will never, ever forget. I came drifting down along the mud and the duckboards—and nothing was happening.

We'd had baked salmon loaf with dried onions in it, which our mess hall specialized in. (Spam was our Sunday meal when we were lucky.) This baked salmon loaf came from this Class-D recycled salmon that they were going to use for fertilizer down in Mississippi, and somebody said, "Ship it to the army," so we got it. And we had the other specialty of the house, which was pickled beets. Baked salmon loaf, pickled beets, and purple Kool-Aid—

better known to the company as Purple Death. I think this drink was some experimental Kool-Aid flavor like fermented raisins, and we got the whole shipment.

So Company K was letting its meal ferment. I came drifting down the company area and there was my little tent, which I shared with five other guys. One of those parameter, six-man tents. It was kind of a cool, fall day, a day like any other day. At that time I'd been in the army—oh, a hundred or a hundred and fifty years and I had maybe another two hundred years to go. So there was no pressure. Nobody was working. Nobody was buckin' for nothin'! 'Cause there was nothing to buck for. As a matter of fact, in our entire tour of duty, our company had only three stripes that were distributed. One guy made Pfc and another guy made corporal. And that was the entire TO. Outside of Lieutenant Cherry and the toadies he had working for him including exec officer, and then, of course there was Sergeant Kowalski, who had every known stripe that was ever given to man. In fact, he was the only nine-striped sergeant I ever saw. He had stripes that went up around the back of his neck and started down the other arm. Old Kowalski and everybody else had disappeared that night—there was just us, the EM.

I got to my tent and went in. You had to bend your head down a little bit, and it was dark. I sat down on the edge of my bunk. I could taste the salmon loaf. It came up a little bit—*ahuh*—like that. There was always an encore—*ughh*—another one would come, and that would be the beets. And then *aghghhhh*—up would come the Purple Death. And then you'd repeat the sequence—go back to the salmon loaf again. And once in a while you'd play a little encore from yesterday, so you get a little SOS in there. Maybe a little dried scrambled eggs. In fact, our company was so poor at times, they couldn't even afford the water for the dried scrambled eggs and we used to spoon in the dried egg powder dry in the morning.

So I'm sitting there on the edge of my bunk. You see what happens in the army—or anyplace, even in college—long stretches where your mind entirely turns off. Your mind has left for Alaska. In fact it's not even there anymore. Your mind is dead—it's gone. Nothing. Your body is just sitting there. You're not even conscious of your body. You're just sort of sitting, see, you're almost approaching one of the rare lotus positions of the true nothingness of being. Your body's not worth looking at now since it's filled with salmon meatloaf. Your mind has been out to pasture now for—oh, ever since the time you got out of basic.

You're sitting there. And I dimly perceive, across the room from me in the darkness is Gasser, sitting on the edge of his bunk. And he is picking his toes. This is a hobby that a lot of guys pick up. You just sit there and pick at your toes. That's kind of nice. You have to do something.

And Edwards is sitting over there on *his* bunk and he's doing what he always did—which is polish his belt buckle. He went through twenty or maybe thirty belt buckles. Just polished them down to the quark stage. Just polished them.

We're sitting there, the three of us. Well, in walks Elkins, the company driver, who is a troublemaker. Elkins is a troublemaker because a long time before, Elkins had seen a Preston Foster movie about how you should join the air force and become a cadet, and he went down and he joined up, and ten minutes later they found out that he didn't have any depth perception, and they just threw him into the big hopper and he wound up driving a half-track. And a half-track ain't exactly a P51 Mustang. He always wears the air force's gung-ho peaked cap and he always sees himself as driving a P51 when he drives the half-track around.

Elkins says, "What time is it? Any of you guys know what time it is?"

Gasser looks up and says, "What difference does it *make*?"

Elkins says, "What do you mean 'what difference'? It makes the difference 'cause I asked. That's what difference it is. I asked what time it is."

I look up from my navel contemplation. I can see that Zinsmeister has now ceased to look up through the hole in the ceiling which he always looks up through when he has nothing better to do. And Edwards has laid his belt buckle down.

Gasser says, "If I told you what time it is, Elkins, would it make any difference?"

Elkins sits down on a footlocker. He says, "What's eatin' you? I said, 'What time is it'"

Gasser says, "What is time, Elkins?"

Elkins says, "What do you mean, 'What is time,' Gasser? Time is whether it's eight-thirty or not."

With that, Zinsmeister—and this is a fatal mistake—Zinsmeister sticks his oar in. "Now, wait a minute. There are several theories about time, men. As a matter of fact, time, according to many philosophers, does not exist at all."

Elkins says, "Are you putting me on? I said, 'What time is it?' Are you trying to tell me that eight o'clock don't exist?"

And Zinsmeister says, "That is correct."

With that, sitting over in the far corner, Goldberg says, "What are you guys talking about? What do you mean time doesn't exist? Time *does* exist! If I can tell you it's eight o'clock, then it's eight o'clock. And if I feel it's eight o'clock, then it's eight o'clock!"

And Gasser says, "Get out! After all, what is time? You got a sun moving around, right? You got an Earth moving around the sun. And somebody, sometime, decided that if we mark off little lines, that would be what time it is."

And Elkins says, "I want to know what time it is. Is it eight-ten or eight-fifteen? What time is it? 'Cause I don't want to miss that crummy show down at the PX!"

Gasser says, "You're an idiot. It's not at the PX, it's at the post theater."

Edwards says, "Now look, you're getting me all confused."

Zinsmeister says, "Some people feel that time does not exist."

And Gasser says, "What do you mean does not exist? Of course it exists. But this fool over here says it's all in my own mind."

And Goldberg says, "That's right, it's all in your own mind."

Elkins gets up and takes ahold of Gasser's shoulder and pushes him flat on the bunk. He says, "Tell me what time it is, fink!"

Gasser gets up and says, "What did you say? I tell you that time is only a thing that is in your own mind."

With that, Elkins hits him in the mouth.

Seconds later, all six guys are rolling on the floor, flailing away. Zinsmeister knocks the tent's stove over, three of the footlockers spill open, Gasser's got a bloody nose, Elkins has got a black eye, and Sergeant Kowalski appears and is pulling them all apart.

Kowalski says, "What's goin' on here, mens? What's going on here?"

With that, Gasser says, "We're trying to decide what time is."

I just wanted to tell you, friends, that that argument was never resolved. And for two years after that it simmered like a terrible fester under the surface of Company K's placid exterior. What is time? Is it on Gasser's Mickey Mouse watch, or is it in Elkins' poor, sad, disappointed mind? Is it in Zinsmeister's contemplation of the eternal hourglass, or is it part of the quark theory of the quantum, dipole-estrogen theory of multiple, fourth-dimensional, time-curve-space-factors? Who is to know?

CODE SCHOOL

I was with a group of guys who were suddenly transferred out of the field that they had been in for a couple of years—radar. We were old, veteran radar. Some of the guys had been overseas for three years and other guys had been overseas for two years and they had ribbons and badges and they were highly trained in all this highly technical equipment, when one day, because of one of those little mistakes that happen when people are operating copy machines at army headquarters, my little group was removed suddenly from its familiar field and was sent to "Classification."

They sent us to a place where new army guys were being processed. How this had happened is a long story, but suddenly we found ourselves being classified as rookies! And so we're all sitting there, glaring.

There were three Pfcs sitting in front of us and they were asking, "Well, what do you want to be in the army?" It's like taking you from your office at BBD&O after nine years and all of a sudden you come there one morning and they had taken all the signs down so it didn't say BBD&O anymore. You walk into your office and there are three guys sitting there at desks, and as you come in they say, "Sit down, fella." What do you mean? I'm vice president in charge of the pickle account! "Sit down, fella! Sit down! We'd like to ask you now, what would you like to do in life? What kind of job would you like to have? We're going to give you some forms, some questionnaires, we're gonna give you a few tests and we'll decide what you guys can do. Some of you might become ditch diggers, some of you might go out and work in a pencil factory." You'd be shocked.

There were about thirty-eight of us and we were sitting in this insane moment and we couldn't believe it. This can't happen. This is not happening at all! Guys kept looking at each other. And these *smug* Pfcs who were up there and had been classifying rookies for years. They sat there and they had their sharp creases and their starched shirts. They were cadre. "All right now, we're going to begin alphabetically. Adams, is there Adams here? Adams? You go over there and sit with Pfc Anderson. We will decide what you're going to do in the army."

And all the while the radio was playing, and coming out of it was a public service announcement. The announcer was saying, "Yes, friends, if you have any special training in electronics, if you're interested in amateur radio operation, if you have any training in radio, the armed forces needs you in the new, secret work going forward in radar. Yes, there is a desperate need for radar technicians. Sign up now. Radar technicians are needed this very moment." Here we were, thirty-eight radar technicians all sitting there and we're in the middle of a classification center and they're trying to decide what we're gonna do!

Well, Gasser, who was sitting in the front said to the Pfcs, "Hey, fellows, listen to what the guy's saying. Hear that? Why don't I just go down and quit and go back out and reenlist, huh? I'll reenlist and become—what are they—radar guys?" Gasser had at least fifteen MOSs. That means the army equivalent of degrees of training after his name, in the field of radar. I had about nine and a half.

And the announcer is saying, "Yes, if you would like to enlist in that fascinating new field called radar, if you have any training in radio, please get in touch immediately. Your country needs you.

Right now we need rad..." and the guys up there were deciding whether or not we were going to be latrine orderlies. "There's a big school we're opening up to teach guys how to type on L. C. Smith typewriters, there's a whole bunch of things opening. You never know what exciting things might open up. We've got a wire school that'll teach you how to solder wires together." Ohhh! Like in Kafka, we knew we weren't going to get out of this.

They were going to send us to school, after we've been in the army a minimum of two years apiece. And so finally Gasser said to a Pfc, "All right, excuse me, Pfc, what's the longest course?"

"What's the longest course? What's that got to do with it?"

"Well, if this insanity is going to go on, I might as well take the longest course. You got one that lasts four years so I can at least stay in New York? I don't care what it is—plumbing—I don't care. What you want."

The private said, "All right, smart guy!" All thirty-eight of us were assigned to the code school at Fort Monmouth, New Jersey.

***

I have to explain that there are two types of code classes. One is for the "high-speed operator," used for transatlantic high-speed operation, and there's what they call "low-grade field operator." Well, the low-grade field operator is the guy in war movies that you see in the shell hole with the rocks and the dirt coming down on him, and all the shrapnel. He's got a little key and he is sending SOS in code when the battalion is cut off and they don't want to use voice transmissions. That had a particular connotation for us and it wasn't that we were afraid of this. It was as though we were nuclear physicists being trained to be file clerks. Oh, we were bugged! Mad! And so we sat in our little cubicles getting an orientation lecture. The code school at Fort Monmouth. Unbelievable.

For those who don't know what code is, I will demonstrate: *dit dit dit dah dah dah dit dit dit.* That's SOS. Have you ever wondered what they send in the movie newsreels? They send "News news news news news" over and over again. That's what the code says. So there I was. I'm a code man and I'm at my apex. I can send and receive code at a minimum of forty-five words a minute. At least seventy-five percent of the thirty-eight guys I was with could send and receive *faster* than any of the guys they had teaching at the code school.

Back at the barracks we sat there glumly, thinking about tomorrow when classes started, but the one thing we did not want to let them know was that we could do it. You know, it's funny. There's always one guy in the crowd who's the catalyst. One guy in the crowd who causes the crowd to go down to city hall. The rest of them may want to do it, but it takes that catalyst, that one guy who says, "Let's go down now. I'm going!" Then the whole crowd goes. That catalyst is important. So, whoever that guy was, finally one of us said, "Ain't gonna get no code outa *me*!" He had said it for all of us.

The next morning, after we had all tacitly agreed there was going to be no code learned in this crowd, we arrived at the code school. The building was three stories high. It covered a full block. You never saw anything like it. There were thousands of guys, all sitting there with earphones in little cubbyholes. All the way up to the top floor, the various speed levels went. On the top floor the finished product was sitting there with typewriters, typing like a high-speed operator, knocking it off at fifty-five words a minute. Way down on the ground floor, guys like us were beginning to learn the alphabet.

Each little detachment went through the whole thing as a unit, providing all the men learned code at roughly the same speed, and each group had a name. Our little band of thirty-eight guys they named "Class D-2." They had these gigantic paper thermometers on the walls that showed how all of the groups were progressing, and there was D-2, its little red dot down at the bottom.

I remember the introductory remarks by the instructor coming through our earphones. Very official. "Men, you are about to learn code, CW, continuous wave transmission. This is one of the most honored methods of man in our day and time, to communicate. Ships have communicated this way now since the early 1900s. You are beginning to learn some of the romance of radio communication. And now, good luck, men, and let's see which detachment gets to the top first!"

All of us in Class D-2 sat there. All of us were high-speed operators, guys who had built transmitters, the whole scene. We were sitting there. The instructor began and we heard the little electronic dots and dashes: *Dit dah dah dit dit dit.* "You have just heard the first two letters of the alphabet, A and B. Then we move on to C and then D and E and F and G, et cetera. As you identify the letters, write them down on the pad in front of you. You will find a pencil to your right." That's like fifteen famous surgeons all sitting down and somebody saying, "You are going to learn how to use a Band-Aid. The Band-Aid is a basic type of bandage."

I listened and I scratched my head. Ow, ah, ah, that must be a D, and I wrote it down. All the while the corporal in charge of our section kept walking back and forth looking at us: "No, no, no, no, now listen carefully." At first he thought we were really trying. "Now listen, fella, now here, all of you fellas, at ease! Turn off your earphones. Fellows, you must listen. Don't listen for dots and dashes, fellows, listen for dits and dahs. Dit dah, it is not dot dash. So A goes dit dah, B goes dah dit dit dit. I think that's where the confusion has fallen. Some of you guys aren't listening right, okay? Start again. All set now, we'll start at the beginning. Dit dah." And thirty-eight guys are just scratching. Some are writing down E, other guys are writing down B. And he's walking around.

"Wait a minute, fellows," he says, "maybe you're nervous. Take a five-minute break, five minute break. All go out for a smoke. You're nervous. Relax, look up at the clouds, take it easy. Five-minute break. Okay, fellows, be back in five minutes."

Five minutes later we were back, and it goes dah dit dah dit. Oh, that's an A. I got it. Finally it's coming out. "It's an A!" When the first day passed, I don't think one of us had written down one single, correct letter.

The next day, all of the nine groups that had started together had little red marks that had moved up on our thermometer, except our little band of malcontents that was still at zero. The others had risen past the four-words-per-minute line. They were moving on to the next tables. By the end of the third day we had painfully progressed roughly to the letter M and the rest of the groups that had started with us were already up on the next floor. And our corporal was saying, "Now look, fellows, look, look, you're not *listening* right. It's all a matter of your head! Your head! You gotta *think* code! You can't think letters, you can't write them, you gotta think code. Look, dah dah is M. Write the first thing that comes into your head, because you'll be right!" He paused. "Okay, let's start the tape. All right, Charlie, start the damn thing again." And our heads were bent over, sweating.

About a week and a half later, and already you can see the big thermometer showing D-1, which was the detachment just ahead of us, was now up at fifteen words a minute. They were the top one. C-1 was down around ten words a minute. A-2 was up to about nine and a half words a minute. Guess where D-2 was? We were still at the starting line!

You never saw such acting. If you think Paul Newman is an actor, if you think Rod Steiger can act, you oughta see thirty-eight GIs refusing to learn code! I never saw such great acting in my life. Gasser, for example, was the *picture* of concentration. Breaking his pencil—"Hold it, my pencil broke!" And I could see poor old Weber sweating. Don Weber was a high-speed operator able to take forty-five words a minute with only one hand on the typewriter. He could take sixty words a minute even getting up and walking around, the code coming in. That kind of guy. You ought to see him really do it. But in this class he was beautiful on the letter C. He kept confusing it with the letter Q.

Well, about twelve days after our little group had started, in came the major. I'll never forget this. What a beautiful morning it was! We were all bent over our desks and we were still sweating over dit dah, dah dit. "All right, you guys, listen," said the major, "you gotta listen! You gotta listen to the corporal. Dah dit is N. Dit dah is A. It's the opposite! All right, now try it again. Send an N, will you, Charlie." Dah dit. "That's an N, not an A! You heard me say N!"

All of a sudden all of our earphones went dead and we saw this enraged look. This major had been an old army ex-first sergeant, who had been made a captain the minute the bombs fell at Pearl Harbor. That old army ex-first sergeant was now in charge of the code school, and he had run into his first problem.

He stood up there, wearing his hat sideways, the collar kind of rolled up, he had that little silver major's leaf hanging down over one ear. He was that kind of officer. He had a shirt on that was a little sweaty, and he hollers, "I'm Major Abromowitz and I can teach code to a dog. I can teach it to a dog! All you guys are goofing off. You're gonna get in trouble with me, and nobody's ever gonna say that Major Abromowitz couldn't teach code to no detachment, you hear that? You hear that? All right, start them code machines!"

Dit dah. Thirty-eight guys write down N. Dah dit dah dit. E.

"All right, you guys," said the major. "You're not gonna git smart with me. I can teach code to a dog! You know what I'm gonna do? I'm gonna transfer every last one of you guys to radar! And you know how hard that is! Boy, are you guys gonna sweat when you get into a radar class. Try goofin' off in that one!"

T/5

I have been made a T/5. For those of you who are technically minded regarding the various ranks in the army, who know the order and chain of command, the T/5 is *almost* a corporal. Not quite. He's *technically* a corporal but they give him no command whatsoever, because they don't think he can be a *real* corporal. But for what he does, he should get a little more money because he works with soldering irons or something like that.

So they give him a corporal's stripes with a T under it, which says, "Don't believe anything this guy says." If a Pfc tells him to go to hell, and the corporal says, "Wait a minute!" and points to the stripes, the Pfc can laugh if it's got the T under it.

So I have made T/5. It's been roughly two and a half years of hard struggle. And I have done it all, man. I have seen the inside of so many grease traps, I know intimately every job that can conceivably be performed in every mess hall from here to—quite probably New Guinea. I'm a hard-bitten soldier and I know damn well where the body lies in every conceivable direction.

PART FOUR

AN ARMY EDUCATION: INDEPENDENT STUDY

*J*ean Shepherd practices radar techniques in the tropics, where he is touched by a bit of the real war—an enemy sub and an Allied freighter off the Florida coast are more than just two blips on the radar screen.

Beyond those particulars, he also describes to us here a variety of experiences that are common to most soldiers anywhere and any time, and Shepherd knows how to tell us about them. There is life in camp and out in the field, life on a pass and life on troop-train rides. Life in the mostly familiar world of millions of other GIs who spend their payday much as Shepherd and Gasser do near Fort Monmouth, New Jersey. What is frustrating about that half-day off with money burning holes in their pockets, is that Shepherd never reveals, regarding a sinister rumor, what calamity awaits Company K, and why he and Gasser got to the front of the line to get their cash. Life in the army is full of such unexpected disasters and mysteries. Shepherd lets them stand as part of life's great unknowns.

By the time Shepherd is telling us about his final days in these last chapters of his army life on the home front, he begins to learn a bit about the enemy. To his surprise, he finds that the POWs he encounters are not the faceless monsters he had imagined. Just like his own comrades in arms, they too are a country's youth, living— enduring—in a world they never made. He will never be able to look at "the enemy" the same way again.

—EB

CASUAL COMPANY EDUCATION

There I was. I was a cool eighteen, and life was a blank slate. Of course I was not aware of that. I thought that the slate was heavily written with deep and profound thoughts, all of which I had arrived at independently. Of course, with the exception of the *present* generation which *has* arrived at all these thoughts independently, and which are profound.

Here I was, hanging around the company area. I had learned many things. For one thing, I had enriched my vocabulary tremendously. I had heard words used in ways that I did not *imagine*, before my entry into the army, could conceivably be used this way. In fact, enlarging your vocabulary often means actually reducing the number of words used—but using them with great care, expressiveness, and with full knowledge of their ramifications and multiple meanings. There was a time it would take me fifteen or twenty minutes to say something, but I learned in the army that I could say an entire thought using two words, over and over again. In fact, I was once in a company where I got the most fantastic educational experience I ever had in my life.

I was in transit one time, and thus detached from my unit, all by myself, and that makes you feel very vulnerable. This is why guys get to have a certain attraction to, and about, and loyalty to, their unit, because in your unit it's like a family. You know where you are. But if all of a sudden you're sent on detached duty and you're sent to about fifteen different casual companies where you have no place, nothing, you get very nervous.

So one day I woke up in a company that I had arrived in at two o'clock in the morning the night before. All by myself in a jeep driven by an angry corporal. The rain pouring down on us, and we arrived at these darkened tents and the guy said, "There's number eight."

Each tent had a whitewashed number on the side of it. Big numbers. I'm not used to this kind of thing, where the numbers are real big. First time I ever ran into numbers on tents. I should have suspected something. I said, "Is that it?"

He said, "Yeah, what the hell are you waitin' for, I don't have all night." You know, this is casual talk in the army. You don't hear this kind of stuff in army movies, where it's always buddies together: "Hey, you wanna see my picture of my girl?" That never really happens.

He said, "What are you waitin' for? Come on, move, will you, buddy!"

So I used the phrase which I'd learned to use so well in the army at that time. It refers to a certain celebration celebrated by my buddies every week. It's "Something your buddies week."

I dragged my barracks bags out of the back of the jeep in the heavy, driving rain and I got into the tent. There were five guys sleeping in it, so there was an empty bunk. Somebody had stolen the blankets off of it, there was no mattress or anything. I threw my bags up on it and I went down to the orderly room, which was lit, and there was a corporal sleeping there behind the desk.

I said, "Ahem, Corporal."

He looked up at me, just looked.

I said, "I'm in eight and there ain't no blanket on my bunk in eight."

At which point, he used the phrase which I had used to the jeep driver, so I knew I was getting no blanket from this guy that night.

I drifted back to tent eight and decided to sleep under my barracks bags since it was now twenty degrees. I put one over my feet and the other over my chest and put my raincoat over it all.

About eight milliseconds after I'd laid down, *kapowwwwww*! A big cannon went off and the walls of the tent shuddered from the crash and I staggered up and heard in the other five bunks these muffled curses. Another bright day had begun. Of course it began in Stygian darkness. It was 4:10 A.M., the hour for reveille in this company. At that point on came a tape bugle that played reveille and then "Stars and Stripes" at eight million watts of audio. The tent was rocking from the vibrations.

I got up in the darkness, and, of course, I was totally dressed. So I didn't have to put on anything. I discovered everybody else in the tent was dressed, it was so damned cold in the tent. Guys went seven or eight years in that company, never took their shoes off.

We went staggering out into the company street in the dark. I saw a huddled figure, the company sergeant working at a clipboard with a flashlight, and he started hollering out names: "Adams," and you heard, "Yo." "Baker," "Yo." "Charlie," "Yo."

He went along and he came to my name and said, "Shepherd," and I said "Yo." He paused. He walked up to me with his light and he shined it in my face. He said, "Aha! I want a good look at you." What the hell have I done?!

He went back to the front of the company and kept going to the last man. Then he hollered, "Company, attention! Right face. Forward harch!"

We marched toward the mess hall, which consisted of a long shed that was darkened, for want of blackout curtains. Dark, dingy, and you could smell the frying kerosene, which, by the way, was a very popular frying oil used in the army, especially on days when we had what was called, euphemistically, French toast. The army knew how to make French toast to fit every taste. One half of each slice was burnt and the other half was raw. So if you liked it in between, you were set.

We were near the mess hall and I was looking around. I couldn't figure out what kind of company this was. A wholly alien company and these guys didn't say anything. The only thing they said was an occasional, ancient Anglo-Saxon word. It was all I heard—all the time. And I heard it used many ways. And here I thought that after a year in the army I *knew* how to use these phrases. But this crowd—they were all artists, every last one of them. And they didn't talk to each other, they just sort of stayed isolated and muttered. Constantly.

We were moving along in the line toward the front door and the guy behind me kept nudging me in the back. Got a bayonet on his belt and he kept hitting me with it—and I knew what kind of company I was in now! *And I turned around*, and before I could say the phrase, he said it to me. All right. So then I started hitting the guy ahead of me with my helmet between his shoulder blades. This was a *real* friendly company. We finally get into the mess hall and I sat down at one the tables, like picnic tables, with benches for five guys on each side. There were plates and bowls turned down for each place. There on top of my overturned cereal bowl was a little box of Wheaties. A single serving box of Wheaties. Everybody had a box of Wheaties on his bowl and they had a big pitcher of milk down the other end of the table.

At that point, the corporal in charge of the mess hall said, "All right, you guys." First mess hall I ever saw where nobody said anything. They were silent. Like being in a prison. He said, "All right, you guys—*EAT!*"

There was a KP coming down the aisle with a great big tray of French toast, and I start to reach for my Wheaties and somebody gave me a shot on the back from the next table. I turned around and he gave me a mean look and he gave me a shot in the liver, I'll tell you! And I said all right—what you usually say in an army mess hall to this guy—and he said it back, with a different inflection. Then I turned back and my box of Wheaties was gone! Somebody had stolen my breakfast!

Here were nine impassive faces looking at me. Have you ever been in a place that was so mean, where they stole your breakfast?! I can understand a watch, your socks even, but your breakfast! So I looked at the five guys looking opposite me, just sitting there with their crew cuts looking mean, and I hunched over my bowl and I reached over and before anybody could do anything, I grabbed the pitcher of milk. I just grabbed it, and I poured the pitcher of milk into my bowl, poured it in and drank it without letting go of the pitcher. I poured it in again. I drank another bowl of milk. A guy down the end said, "Pass the milk." At which point I used the word gain—to describe what he should do to himself.

It was an impasse. It was ten mean people, tough, mean people. Don't think for a minute I'm Woody Allen, I was hard as a rock and twice as mean. The ten of us just sat there. Finally I just took the milk and shoved it to the guy next to me, I shoved it in his gut. "Here's your milk." At which point he answerd me in kind. The same word. We sat there during the entire breakfast conversing in Anglo-Saxon phrases.

I spent one week in that company and every night the NCOs would go around with flashlights and look under the mess hall for guys who had gone AWOL. That kind of company. Mean.

And it turned out it was a group of GIs who had been taken out of stockades all over the world, who were illiterate and who were being taught to read. That's why they had the big 8. They couldn't read a little 8, they had a big 8. Instructors said, "8. Put up 1, 2, 3, 4 fingers. You put up 4 fingers on the other hand and that's the 8. That's where you sleep." Little had I realized that when I'd landed in that company they couldn't read and that was why the guy stole the box of Wheaties. He didn't know it was Wheaties. It was just a box of something. Could have been anything—full of wrist watches. Ohhh! The army is educational, friends.

PRIVATE SANDERSON

In the Army you get to meet such a fantastic cross-section of people that you would never choose to have anything to do with. One time I was in a "casual company," which is a little this side of purgatory, very closely allied with some of the more esoteric sections of Hell. A casual company is where they've thrown all the castoffs, for one reason or another, into this barracks together. They come from diverse backgrounds and there's nothing that holds them together except that they're in Casual Company C, 4132 Signal Airborne Mess Kit Repair Battalion. They're in the army, that's about all.

And I have this double-deck bunk, and I have the bottom, see. The top bunk is vacant and they've got the mattress rolled up and back, so for about the first two or three days in the casual company, I'm lying there on my sack, and I can see the ceiling through the springs of the top of the bunk and I can smell the butt cans and once in a while I hear a company go by and a truck going by. In an Army movie or short story you never get a sense of the sounds that you have in an Army camp. The continual sound of prime movers going by, *AAAHHGRRRRRRRGHAAAA!* Once in a while you hear *MROOOOOMMM!*, an airplane goes over that shakes the roof. They don't have the same noise abatement laws in the Army that govern Queens.

I'm lying in my sack one day in the casual company and I'm goofing off a little bit. I'm supposed to be somewhere—latrine orderly or something, and you can hear Company M taking a little drill out there in the back, and this guy comes in through the barracks door with barracks bags over his shoulder with stuff falling out of them and his hat's on sideways and his ears are bent over on both sides of it. He's a short, squat guy, he looks sort of like a fire plug with feet. That kind of guy. There's a certain kind of guy in the army, no matter what he's wearing he looks sloppy. Everything's all rumpled. You hear about guys polishing their brass—forget it—this guy has a belt that was all twisted into a knot. Just a rotten, crummy soldier. He comes walking in and looks around the barracks and sees this empty bunk. Well, there I am lying flat on mine and looking up at the ceiling. I hear the jeep pulling away—they brought him down from the gate someplace and he's been cast off by some company. You can see a couple of little threads sticking off of his sleeve where the Pfc stripe has been torn off.

He looks down at me and says, "Hey, mac," with a kind of Southern accent. Almost every outfit I've ever been in in the army is vaguely Southern.

I say, "Yeah?"

"Hey, mac, is that bunk there empty?"

I say, "Yup."

He comes clumping down and he takes his barracks bags and throws them up on the top bunk and he goes stomping out. In about three minutes the screen door slams again and he comes in with a pile of blankets and sheets and a pillow from the supply room and he makes his bed.

He says nothing whatsoever. He's standing right next to me and I'm looking at him. You can see it's impossible to even conceive of his pants ever having been pressed. The legs are round. In fact he has little bags where his knees are. The bottom of his GI pants are frayed. Who knows what Hell this guy's been through. And he's saying nothing. Little, short, squat sort of blond guy, red-faced and his hat on sideways. He's the kind of guy who, no matter how recently his shirts have come back from the cleaners, their collars are curled up. And he's got this GI tie that's all knotted and sweaty and it's got crud all over it and it kind of hangs down. He shimmies up the side of the bed and now he's in the sack. It's bulging down up above me, and we're saying nothing.

All of a sudden the squawk box opens up and it says, "Sanderson, come up to the orderly room right away. Sanderson in Barracks B. Sanderson."

I hear the bunk above me squeak and this guy opens up with an epithet. He just lets it go! In a rich, Southern, lower Tennessee drawl. This is a two-way squawk box that you can talk back to and they hear you.

"What was that?!"

And he repeats it!

"Who said that?"

And there is a pregnant pause and he says, "You guess."

"I'm coming right down there!"

Oh, no! I've been having a nice afternoon lying here and this guy comes in and he's not here three and a half minutes and we have tangled with you-know-whats in the orderly room. For crying out loud, I'm not going to be caught here in my bunk, so I get up instantly and I go scurrying toward the back of the barracks trailing underwear and shoes. And as I go tearing toward the door the guy's looking at me and he says, "Chicken!"

I hide back of the latrine for a while till I figure it's cooled off and I look in the barracks and I see this guy Sanderson lying in his bunk. I don't know what's happened with the orderly room, but obviously it's all over. So I come sneaking back and I crawl back into my bunk and I lie down and neither one of us says a word.

All of a sudden I hear this sound above me. It is a sound that's indescribable. Suffice it to say it's a kind of throaty upheaval up there. The bunk jiggles a bit and right past my ear goes the biggest gob of tobacco juice that I have ever seen. The size of a moderately small football. It goes whistling right past my ear and lands right smack on my footlocker!

The battle was joined. I mean, anybody that spits tobacco juice on your footlocker—chewing tobacco! There's this old army trick. I'm lying in the bottom bunk and I take my foot and I place it right on the bunk above and push up hard! And this guy goes up. You can see him heave and there's this scrunching sound and he comes flying off the bunk and lands flat on his face right in between the two bunks. He gets up and says, "Why'd you do that for?"

I say, "You spit tobacco juice on my footlocker."

"Was that your footlocker? I thought that was the footlocker that belongs to the guy in the next bunk!"

I say, "Would that have made a difference?"

He says, "Sure, I never spit on a bunkmate's footlocker."

Ah! The unspoken code of the army! There is honor among thieves. I say, "Oh, in that case, okay. Just clean it up."

So he takes one of his army socks. He's got a lot of his laundry lying out on top of his bunk. He takes one of his socks and it's one of his clean socks and he just brushes off the tobacco juice. Just brushes it all off. He sticks it back up there with the laundry.

Well, that night we take off to go down to the mess hall to eat. Me and Sanderson go down together. I know not one single person in the casual company and the only guy that I've known anything at all about is Sanderson. We get at the end of the chow line and we see that way up ahead they are serving tonight, fried chicken. So he turns to me and says, "What you bet they're gonna run out before we get up there."

I say, "Why do you say that?"

"They always do."

We see every guy up ahead peeling off and they've got this great big half a fried chicken with the cranberry sauce and all the fixings. Sure enough, three guys ahead of us, the cook comes out, takes the empty tray back and he lays out the cold cuts.

Sanderson takes one look at the cold cuts and he says, "Hey! Hey, buddy." He's talking to the mess sergeant. This is some imposing mess sergeant. And Sanderson says, "Hey buddy, you don't expect me to eat that—" and he uses an expression for cold cuts that you will never hear outside of the army.

The mess sergeant turns around and says, "What'd you say? Who said that?" And who do you think he's looking at? Guess who!

I say, "I didn't say nothin'. Not me! A ... a ... I like salami and baloney."

"Don't give me that. What did you say?"

Sanderson's saying nothing. Then he says, "What's a matter, are you afraid to tell him you said it?"

You son of a ..., I think. What are you trying to do? Now I'm in trouble with the mess hall!

We hurry along and pick up our silverware and I look at my plate. They always cut the baloney about four inches thick. There's something about baloney when it's nice and thin and on a sandwich, it's *right*, but when it's four inches thick and it comes with sort of lukewarm broccoli that's been boiled for seventeen straight hours and in addition to that you have flat apple pie with grape Kool-Aid, it isn't a meal that exactly sings.

We start to walk back through the mess hall. All the guys are sitting there and you can see the chicken bones piled up and they've got the cranberry sauce, and we're coming back with cold cuts. About halfway through the mess hall Sanderson turns around.

"Hey, whatta you say we go down to the PX? Get something really to eat, huh?"

I say okay and we walk up to the chow line where guys are handing it out and he just takes his tray and dumps it in the uneatable garbage. They've got two garbage cans, the eatable and the uneatable and he's dumped it in the uneatable, and with that, the mess sergeant says, "Hey, you, come here, mac. You see that sign up there?" The sign says TAKE ALL YOU WANT. BUT EAT ALL YOU TAKE. "Where are you throwin' that? Do you know that a whole family in Bulgaria can live on that for a week?" And Sanderson looks at him and says, "Then why don't you go to Bulgaria and give it to 'em? Don't you hand me that!"

<hr />

So now we're out in the cold air. I'm with my *friend*, Sanderson. The first true primitive. Now you would never meet this kind of guy in ordinary life. I would have nothing to do with him. I just wouldn't know him. We're walking along toward the PX and he's chewing a big chew of Sweet Apple Cut Plug, and he's spitting on the shoes of people going by.

I say, "Hey, Sanderson, what's your MOS?"

"My what?"

"Your MOS?"

"521. I'm a rifleman."

"You're what?!"

"I'm a rifleman."

We walk along further. He's what they call cannon fodder. He's the Good Soldier Schweik. He is the basic material of which all armies are made and have been made ever since the days of Hannibal. I suppose that there were four guys named Sanderson sitting about three or four elephants from the rear when Hannibal was going over the Alps and they all sat there with their shovels and complained about this general. He's the universal soldier.

So we walk along on our way to the PX and I say, "When you get drafted?"

"Weren't drafted."

"How'd you get in?"

"I joined up."

"Joined up? How come?"

"Why not?"

"I could think of a lot of reasons why not."

"Well, I joined."

"Did you join the reserves or what?"

"Regular."

"You're regular army?"

"Yup."

"How long you been in?"

"Twelve years."

Twelve years! He's in a casual company and an ex-Pfc!

I say, "Gonna stay in?"

"You bet. I found a home."

"You found a home?"

"Yep."

We walk a little further on toward the PX. I'm describing a true, genuine private in the army. This is a genuine, basic private. After casually walking along looking at the scenery, passing the WAC barracks and that kind of stuff, I say, "Hey, Sanderson, what'd you do when you were home?"

"Nothin' much. Worked at a garage."

Yeah? What'd you do?"

"Mess around."

"What do you do in the army?"

"Same thing. Mess around."

"Were you married?"

"Oh, yeah. I was married three times."

"Where?"

"Oh, lots of places. I married a Polack one time in Chicago."

"Oh?"

"Yep."

"Are you married now?"

"No, I thrown her out."

All right. So we walk a little further on. Our conversation is growing richer and deeper by the minute. He says to me, "Want a chaw?"

I say, "A what?"

"A chaw. Here, I got a new pack here." And he reaches in his blouse pocket and on it is a good conduct ribbon, and his good conduct ribbon is all dirty. He won this ribbon years ago, and it's all cruddy, thumbprints and dirt all over it, and he says, "Here, have a chaw."

So I figure I'll be kind of sociable with Sanderson. So I pack this stuff back in my trap and the instant I get it back there I start feeling queasy and sick to my stomach, but I put up with it because I'm out with a tough guy. And along comes a second lieutenant, one of these twelve-year-old ROTC types from Baylor or Texas Christian. Long, thin red neck, very sharp. Their hats fit right on top of their heads. Square. And they've got everything sharp and pressed and pants just a little too short and GI shoes all clean and bright. And he comes walking along and Sanderson throws him a salute that is one of the snottiest—if you can imagine a salute that is somehow properly done but at the same time is an obscene gesture. The second lieutenant looks at him and he recognizes instantly that this is a guy that you're not gonna tangle with. You've seen this in the army. You don't mess around with Sandersons in the army. You just let them go and hope that you don't run into them again.

We get to the PX and we drink a couple of cans of GI beer. We mix that with a couple of malted milks. And that, of course, with the Apple Cut Plug, and we have some Milky Ways and a couple of Powerhouse. A couple of tuna salad sandwiches. This is a typical GI meal down at the PX.

We stand around over at the cash register and talk to the chick who's working over there. Then we're back at our table and we've got cans all around of GI beer. All the while my stomach is getting a little more queasy as time goes by and it's getting late and Sanderson drinks three more 3.2 beers and he's feeling a little good and he's beginning to look for a fight! One of the first things that basic yardbirds do is to look for someone to take it out on. There's two kinds of soldiers. There's the kind of soldier who dedicates his time in the army to staying out of trouble. I'm a very circumspect soldier. Then there's the other kind who dedicates his time in the army to being *in* trouble. And when the two of them get together, man, I want to tell you!

So we're sitting at our table and Sanderson looks over at a Pfc who's chewing away on a tuna fish sandwich and he's got some kind of patch on his shoulder I've never seen before. Sanderson says, "Hey, you. Hey, man, how long you been in the Flyin' Teakettle?"

And this guy turns around. You can see he's been drinking 3.2 beer. Face kind of purple already, and he says, "What'd you say, mac?"

"How long you been in the Flyin' Teakettle? That's the worst damn outfit I ever seed. I was in that outfit once for two weeks. Man, I got out of it. What a piss-poor outfit. Man, I'll tell you that is really chicken! Wow, oh wow! Flyin' Teakettle!"

I can see the patch is really spectacular—wings and a tornado on it and stuff. The guy says, "Listen here. You tryin' to put me on?"

"Puttin' you on? Man, ain't nobody who'd even wear the Flyin' Teakettle patch can be put on, 'cause they's ignorant from the start. That's a dumb outfit."

Question—how many times in your life have you *been* with a provocateur? And *you* got sucked into the maelstrom? You know, being with some slob in a bar who *insists* on starting a fight with somebody. What do you do? How many times have I ridden with cab drivers and they start yelling at some other cab driver out of the window? What do you do? Are you on *his* side? Do you applaud your cab driver? Especially when you know that this son of a gun you're riding with has cut that other guy off seventeen times? What do you do?

So these two guys start a shoving match. A shoving match is not a real fight. "Hey, get out of here!" Shoving. "You say that again!" They're just shoving each other.

All of a sudden in come three MPs, just like that. You don't start this stuff in the PX. "All right you guys, come on, line up over here. Lemme see your ID, come on. Name, rank, what outfit are you from? Come on, mac." All my life I've been keeping out of trouble. So I take out my wallet and there's my little ID and I'm in this casual company and all.

"Okay, all right." They're writing it all down, these guys with the white helmets. Name, rank. Here's Sanderson and he's lovin' it! All of his life he's been in this hassle. This is what the army *is* about to him. This is why he's been in one casual company after another. He's lovin' it. You see the big grin. He's got that big, red-faced grin. All his life he's been hanging around juke joints getting in fights. It's indiscriminate. He fights everybody.

The MP sergeant says, "All right now, give me your name, rank, serial number."

Sanderson says, "Hennessey." He's giving a fake name! "My name is Hennessey, I'm over in the Second Army Headquarters Company, Fourth Battalion."

The sergeant writes it down. "Lemme see your card."

"I don't have it with me."

"Okay," writes it down.

Being *me*, I've given him my right name! There's some guys who can't help being patsies in the world. So I give him my right name!

Now we're out in the night again and Sanderson's in his glory. He's had his little action for tonight and he's had about ten 3.2 beers so he stops off at a latrine. Now we're walking through the darkness. The quiet night. The army is beginning to slowly sink into somnolence. You know that feeling around an army camp. It's around ten-thirty and they're about to blow taps and you can see the lights and you can hear guys playing craps in the dayroom. You hear the pool balls clicking together. We are heading back toward home. The casual company. Home.

We arrive back in the barracks and we're not there five minutes when the PA system calls out, "Shepherd. In the orderly room, right away."

I get up, and Hennessey—we now call him Hennessey, from Second Army Headquarters Company, Fourth Battalion—is now sound asleep in the bunk above me in his uniform with his shoes on. *DZZZZZ.* Every time he snores there's this fine spray of tobacco juice that hangs in the air above him, and the smell of old 3.2 beer and old fistfights that he fought in places all the way from Joplin, Missouri, to Rabbit Hash, Tennessee. He's fistfought his way all through North Africa with the 82nd Airborne. And now here he is snoring away in his bunk, a happy soldier. *DZZZZZ*, that fine spray of tobacco juice. I get up and put on my shoes and there's a long line of bunks with guys sitting there writing letters, other guys are sleeping. And I go down through the darkness and into the orderly room and there sitting is the first sergeant. "Okay, Shepherd, what happened tonight down at the PX? Got a note here from the provost marshal. Who you shovin' around?"

I said, "Who am I shoving around?"

"Yup, we got a note here and you were with some guy from the Headquarters Company, Second Battalion. Somebody named Hennessey. You know anything about him?"

"Yes."

What outfit's he from? Is he from the Second Battalion, Headquarters Company?"

"Yup, he is." I'm perjuring myself! For that clod back there in the barracks! Getting myself deeper into trouble. Because that's part of being a patsy. On the one hand other guys *do it* to you, but you never *quite* have the *guts* to do it to them! And he's back there *DZZZZZ*. He's snoring away back in the barracks.

So I'm standing there in front of that miserable desk in the orderly room. There's something about the yellow light in an orderly room just before taps. The CQ has come in, the guy that's on at night. The first sergeant has been running this casual company with an iron fist for lo these many years. He's had the dregs of humanity go through this outfit. And he's looking up at me. "All right. Tell you what we're gonna do. I don't want to bother the captain with this kind of stuff. Tell you what I'm gonna do. I'm gonna restrict you to seven days to the barracks, to the company area, and I don't want to hear no more trouble out of you, okay?"

"Yes, sergeant."

"I don't want you hanging around with Hennessey. That crowd at Headquarters Company ain't no good. Those guys are professional soldiers. You can get in trouble with them. Okay?"

"Yes, sergeant."

"Now we're not gonna hear more from you, right?"

"Yes sergeant."

"All right, you are now under arrest as of eleven-oh-five. Seven days."

And I walk out into the night. Back to the barracks. I crawl into the bunk. And up above me I can see that bulge hanging down. I can see a pile of socks next to his barracks bag. Pile of underwear. I can see his raunchy fatigues hanging from the rod back of the bunk. He has the raunchiest fatigues. He must have spent five years in the grease trap. He has fatigues that could get up and talk and walk all by themselves at night and go out and have dates with girls. He's lying up above me. The happy soldier's up there. *DZZZZZ.* Another fine mist of *eau de* tobacco juice comes drifting down. *DZZZZZ.* Sleeping up there as happy as a hog in a hog wallow. Which is what he is in a way.

I'm lying in my sack. Seven days under arrest. And it's going to go on my record. Seven days. I ain't gonna leave this barracks. And once in a while they'll take me out and give me something to eat. After everybody else has had the fried chicken, they'll give me a few little chunks of baloney. Some of those Brussels sprouts that I can hardly wait to get at. Lukewarm. Parboiled Brussels sprouts. Maybe they'll even give me a little of that raisin Kool-Aid. Purple Death. Once in a great while they'll come down and take me out with a couple of other guys wearing fatigues to clean out the latrine. With a big thing on the back that says "P." A guy takes you around with a sawed-off shotgun. Yes, sir.

So I'm lying there in the sack. Seven days. And off in the distance someplace is the first sergeant, the old pro. He's going through the morning report already and he's getting ready to turn in his papers. The yellow lightbulb hangs there and army life goes on. Off in the distance you hear the sound of pool balls clicking together. And somewhere off in the way far distance you hear the sound of a radio playing in one of the barracks or in one of the mess halls. It's playing Roy Acuff records. Everywhere you go in the army you hear Elvis Presley, Roy Acuff, you hear the same sound, that constant sound of guys singing through their nose. Singing eternally about lost loves, "Yeah, Ah want you ta tell me, the next time you are goin' ta town. You're slippin' around on me, baby, an' Ah know that you're slippin' ta town. Oh, I was a lonesome soldier in old Korea town."

I'm lying there on the bunk just living the life, playing it cool. Playing it easy. Waiting for Sanderson to wake up. Waiting for something to happen. Seven lonely days and seven lonely nights.

The second day of my internment Sanderson comes ambling in about two o'clock chewin' tabacca. He walks up to the bunk and he pulls down two barracks bags and starts taking off his fatigues and stuffing them in the bag. He has barracks bags that are worn thin from traveling. And he just stuffs his stuff in and I'm lying still on my bunk. Under arrest.

I say, "Where you going, Sanderson?"

"Being shipped."

I say, "Where to?"

"I don' know."

"Where you going?"

"How the hell do I know where Ah'm goin'? I just been shipped. They just cut the orders. I don' know."

"Where do you *think* you're going, huh?"

"Oh, maybe the West Coast someplace. Think Ah'm headin' out for Camp Ord, Ah believe." And he continues to pack. He gets his stuff all packed. Puts on his crummy old uniform, his crummy old GI shoes. He takes down his pictures which he carries around with him and had stuck up back of the bunk. Sticks them into his barracks bag and then, without so much as a goodbye, he flings his bags over his shoulder and starts out.

I say, "Good luck, Sanderson."

"Don't worry, I'll land on ma feet."

I say, "Yes, I know."

He's now almost at the door. And his last words, as he heads out into the shimmering heat are, "Well, hang loose, son. Don't let 'em do it to ya."

~~~~~~~~~

I never see him again. Somehow, someplace, Sanderson is still making the scene. Somewhere, someplace, he's still hanging around a gas station, maybe he's hanging around a diner, maybe he's sitting there listening to Roy Acuff records, telling the guys about the days when he was in the army. Now he's on pension. He's a twenty-year man. He's livin' high off the hog. Sitting there with his cane pole fishing for bullheads. Someplace in southern Tennessee, knocking heads together on Saturday nights when he does a little jukin' them pretty old girls in Nashville. And so I want to salute the basic yardbird, wherever he is. He's not only the *salt* of the earth, he's something *else* of the earth.

MOS: CHICKEN TECHNICIAN

So Shepherd is sitting there, you know. He's been in the army now for about a year and a half or two years. Long enough to know the score. And it's a very subtle score. He's been in the army long enough to know there's basically nothing that you can really count on in a vast organization like this. Yet you can count on certain things. But the things you can count on are not the things you want. Anyone knows, who has been in *any* of the armed forces— the services are different in *detail* but the *same* in total concept.

You're in. That's the total concept. You ain't out—you're in. Big difference. Now what does that mean? When you're in, you can't get out. No matter what you're doing in civilian life, even if you're in eighth grade, there's the secret knowledge that you could quit. Maybe hard, but you could do it. You could pull it off. But I have very rarely seen a guy pull it off in the army—go down to the orderly room and say, "Hey, I've had this, you know. I quit. I'm giving you my two weeks' notice."

One of the great things about being in a situation like that is that you learn to celebrate very small victories. You learn to appreciate tiny things. So a guy sitting on his footlocker in the army does various things to survive. There's the guy who sleeps. In every outfit I've ever seen, there's always one guy in the barracks who figures that if he continues to sleep whenever he can for three years, he will not remember any of it. And he sleeps. You see this bunk down at the end there's this huddled figure—sleeping away. Slept all through it. Then there is the polisher. Some guys just sit on their footlocker and polish their shoes, grimly, endlessly, belt buckles, shoes. This is the way he spends his life. Then there is the letter writer. There are guys who seem to be writing endlessly, endlessly, endlessly. These are sort of gray-type guys. You wonder who the hell is interested in hearing from them, but they write endlessly.

I was another type entirely. I was a mover. A mover is always down trying to get a pass. And somehow keep moving, keep moving, get transferred. My trick was to move fast. Move in the night and apply for a transfer by morning—and be on your way. If you keep moving—keep a moving target—they'll never get you.

Well, one afternoon, our entire Company K, just without any warning at all, was shipped—just like that—*bam*! We came back from the rifle range, it was noon, and posted on the bulletin board it said, "All men will assemble at thirteen-hundred with full field pack, equipment packed, ready to move out by thirteen-fifty. We assumed that this was just one of those little maneuver-type things. Thirteen-fifty arrived and we were all standing around with a hundred pounds of junk on our backs. Trucks pulled up and twenty minutes later we were rolling through the countryside on a train. And everybody was scared. This was serious. We rolled on and on through the night. We rolled on and on and on, through half of the next day. The train pulled into a siding and stayed there, it seemed like ten hours. Then we rolled on again. Always north, always north, and then at 2 A.M. we pulled into the siding of another train station, the doors slammed open, and we were marched out in the five-below temperature, the wind screaming out of the north. Company K knew this was no joke.

And they moved us into more trucks and carried us through the night to a place called the Motor Pool, in a dark, dreary, frozen camp. We were assigned tents which had not been slept in for two and a half years. The six-man parameter tent I was in had a great rip over the top and snow was drifting in. We hadn't seen snow for two years! We'd been down in the tropical swamps. All of a sudden, snow! And here we were lying in our bunks, and I piled everything I could think of on top of me to keep warm. I had my gas mask on to keep my face warm.

At four-thirty in the morning, *poom*! The gun went off and marches were playing over the PA system all over this camp. They woke you up with this fantastic shot in the head and guys were struggling up in the dark and I could hear them lining up in the company street out in front. I lined up in the darkness. We didn't know where we were going, what we're doing. We didn't know what was going to happen. A strange sergeant out in front of us with a clipboard started reading the roll call.

The roll is an important thing in the army. He mispronounced every name—including Smith. You never answer, "Here," in the army because once you answer "Here" in the army you're making a definite statement: You're here! And that's saying that you tacitly approve what's going on—"Here, Shepherd is here." So you don't say that. Everybody has his own technique of answering the roll. Some guys went "Yeah." Other guys went "Ye-ah." The most common type was "Yo," and each guy had his own pitch: "Yo," "Yi," "Yah," "Yu," "Ye."

When he finally ended the roll, he said, "Immediately following noon chow we will have a reclassification program. All you guys who think you've been trained in the army the last two years, we are reclassifying you. How many radar mens we have here in this group? You will be reclassified down at the wire school. How many long-distance telephone operators we got in this group? You will be reclassified at the wire school. Reclassification examinations will begin at fifteen-thirty. Any questions?" Any questions! In that one comment he had just said, "Your entire life is ruined."

The ultimate humiliation was visited upon us. I don't care what you do for a living, friend. What if it's taken you nine years to learn to be a doctor. What if tomorrow morning they lined you up in front of the hospital and a guy got up and said, "All you mens that are doctors here will be reclassified at one o'clock this afternoon. You will be assigned to truck-driver school." My god! All the guys in our company had years of schooling in radar—it was an elite group. All of us had been technicians for two years, working with highly complex equipment—millions of dollars worth of radar. And just with one fell swoop, one swell foop, we were all reduced to basic yardbirds.

Well, we drifted back into the tents. I remember sitting there and saying, "What the hell now?" Well, I'll tell you about mankind. Man is great in one respect. His mind instantly, in spite of disasters, adjusts to a current adversity. That's great! If we didn't, we wouldn't have existed this long. Within five minutes none of us were even thinking of ourselves as radar men anymore. We were basic yardbirds and now the thing to do was hit and land on your feet and work out another good deal. Right away we were planning, we were plotting: "Don't tell 'em you can type, and my god, ever hear about that low-speed code school? I'll tell you what—don't let 'em send you to that. If they give you a code test, you don't know how to take it!

Ten minutes later we were standing out in the cold, the wind blowing, and another guy stepped out in front of us. "I'm Corporal Simonson, your duty corporal. From now on I will assign you to your duties here at your temporary post. You guys from here on down are assigned to the consolidated mess hall. How many of you ever worked in a consolidated mess before?" Nobody wants to admit he's done anything in the army, because the next thing you know you're screwed. A consolidated mess is not the same as a regular mess hall. It's like a big Horn & Hardart in the sky. It serves divisions—everybody on a post goes there and it serves twenty-four hours a day. What does that mean? That means that twenty-four hours a day there are guys scouring pans, twenty-four hours a day there are guys dragging dregs out of oatmeal pots, twenty-four hours a day there are guys doing all the humiliating stuff that goes into preparing food, cleaning up—*oooohhh*!

At the consolidated mess the mess sergeant looked at us all and sent most of the guys back to the kitchen and told Gasser and me, "You two guys are outside men," which is a great deal, because outside men, as an army tradition, just hang around outside the mess hall and talk to people arriving: "Yeah, we got corned beef today, SOS, yeah." That's all. The sergeant said, "You two guys are dismissed. Report back here at twelve noon." Fantastic! Nothing to do until noon. In the army that's incredible. Man, what a victory! Totally unexpected. The unexpected victory is the one that counts!

At noon we were back at the mess hall. A corporal took us back to the kitchen and the rest of our buddies were there, looking at us—"Boy, you two sure got a deal!"

The corporal said, "All right you two, this is why we saved you." He opened the door to the storeroom. I couldn't believe my eyes. The floor of the storeroom, which was about fifteen feet square, was covered with newspapers, and covering the newspapers to at least a five foot height, was a gigantic pile of unplucked, uncleaned, totally, completely dead, very dead chickens. He said, "You guys are gonna clean them chickens."

Then began one of the most educational days of my life. Me and Gasser cleaned four hundred chickens. You have no idea what's in chickens, friends. When you clean four hundred you learn a lot of anatomy. And most of it you don't want to learn.

Four hundred chickens. Even now, at this minute, when I think of chickens, when I walk past the frozen food counter, I don't look at those lovely Frank Perdue, beautifully-cleaned-and-wrapped-in-cellophane breasts, I see something else.

PASSES DENIED

Here we were in Company K, the whole crowd, and we liked our officer. That's the worst part of it—we liked our officer. He was kind of a thin, watery-looking man and he had very sharp, nicely pressed clothes all the time. I imagine he slept in pressed GI underwear. Everything was pressed and so clean, and even his little bars sparkled—I think they had batteries attached to them in his pockets so they'd shine in the dark. His glasses and his eyes sparkled. But something nutty happened to him. He developed a bad tooth or something—I don't know what it was.

I don't know what happened to him. You could almost see him changing. Maybe he heard that Company K had gotten a bad efficiency report. Nothing worse than to have come drifting down from headquarters: "Oh, what a cruddy outfit. Get on the stick, mac."

Well, he began to develop this strange habit. He would call us to attention and stand in front of us and just look. He would walk back and forth and just look. It was very unnerving. It was like if for years your boss is just looking at you as you walk past him in the hall. His eyes follow you. You say, "Ha, ha, ha, Mr. Bullard." He says nothing. "Oh, ha, Mr. Bullard, how are you?" Wouldn't that be an awful feeling? Cold blue eyes. No expression. No anger. Just looked. Well, you could hear all of Company K, standing at attention, two hundred of us, our guts pulled in, sharp, pressed, our buckles shined, our elbows clean, our hats all at the proper angle, our breaths coming in short whistles, standing there. And this guy's just walking around looking at us. Looking. Ten minutes, fifteen minutes, just looking, and all of a sudden he would just nod to the first sergeant, he wouldn't even talk to us anymore, he would just nod and tuck in his head, and the first sergeant would say, "Fall out!"

Before this, we had always broken up really fast, everybody running like at recess, guys hitting each other and yelling, off to the PX. But now we'd mill. There would be little knots of worried guys—"What's going on here? What is it?" Everyone thought that "Somehow, it was *me!*" You always feel this in the army. Somehow that boom is gonna fall. It's gotta hit! I'm gonna get it in the back of the neck. So Gasser said, "Aw, you know, he's an *officer*. He's an officer." No, no, he wasn't. He was a man. And he just kept looking at us. Day after day.

Then one day we shipped. We figured, this was it, we're going overseas. We rode night after night in the train and we finally got to this next camp. We put our stuff in the barracks, got everything packed way, everything was sharp and clean and he called a company formation. And he stood and looked at us. Not saying a word. Just walked around and looked at us.

Now we were under alien skies. There was an unfamiliar battalion across the road from us. There was an unfamiliar company down the company street from us. And they were looking, like somebody new has moved into the neighborhood. You all live in a neighborhood where somebody new moves in and everyone's curious about them. This is the way it is in the army. A new company moves in, a new battalion comes in and everyone's curious. They look down there and they see this funny equipment, crazy-looking tanks they come in with, or the guys have goofy-looking patches, some kind of nutty thing about them. "What kind of an outfit is that? Wow!"

You could see guys looking out of barracks as we were standing at attention, and there was a light snow drifting down. A slow, easy, soft, Robert Frost kind of snow. Just drifting down. It wasn't very cold, it was a beautiful day. And I could see the guy ahead of me had his hat at the proper angle, his coat all sharp and pressed, with the snow just drifting down on his shoulders. We were all standing, watching, waiting. It's the new area and I could see a couple of guys across the company street in the other battalion, the 3174th. They're looking out of the barracks. "What the devil is with that company out there?" There was silence in the street. Nobody saying a word. "What's with that company?" We wished *we* knew.

Just standing. And the captain finally just gave the nod to the first sergeant. The first sergeant said, "All right, you guys. Attention! Fall out!" And he stood and looked at us without a single word. Our old ex-friend just looked and stood.

Well, that night a notice appeared on the bulletin board that there would be no leaves for three weeks. We were detained and we were to be kept in the company area! Do you know what it's like to be in the company area for three weeks? That's like if somebody came to you and said, "You are going to be locked in the john for the next six months. You aren't getting out. You're just going to stand in there. That's it. And all your reading matter is going to be supplied by the Scott Tissue Company. Nothing else. That's it, man. Maybe once in a while you can look out of the window. That's it. Boy, you talk about stir crazy!

We sat in the barracks night after night, we'd go down to the pool table in the dayroom. There were no pool balls. All we had were two cues and the pool table. Guys would take rolled-up pieces of paper to play pool with. That kind of stuff. We had one Ping-Pong paddle. One. Ever try to play a game with one Ping-

Pong paddle? Guys would hit it with their hand, the other guy's got the paddle, using it in his weaker hand. We had all kinds of schemes to handicap. We played craps with one die. No money, of course, because we'd been red-lined for about four months. No money. Just walking around.

Well, the rumor began to circulate around this part of the camp that we were a detention company that was on special probation because we were a bunch of hard apples! I don't know how this started, but they do have those companies in the army where all the tough guys have finally been dragged out of the slam after they've done their six months for killing a first sergeant or stealing a truck or shooting a captain or something like that. They have these companies where they put these guys back in! They put them all in one special company and they have a couple of sluggers who are their officers. Well, the rumor got out and the other companies were watching us and they stayed away. It's like, when the rumor gets out that someone in the neighborhood's got leprosy, you don't come around. Believe me, sin is catching. Crime is catching. Poverty is catching. Bad company commanders are catching. Rottenness is catching, so you don't come around. And guys would give a wide berth right around our company area.

Remember, we couldn't get out of the company area. We couldn't even go to the PX! You know what that means? No Milky Ways! Nothing. You just sat there night after night on your bunk and fistfights would break out. Somebody'd just gotten up and said, "Oh, Yeah?!" Nothing had been said. He just hit a guy in the mouth and everybody applauded. It was the first action in days. Big fistfight going on, and the PA system would open and you'd hear, "Cut it out, you guys!" And then we'd subside for a minute. We'd sit there and somebody would invariably answer the PA, which was an intercom system. Somebody would go,

"*Buckabuckabuckabuckabuck!*" There'd be a silence and then from the PA, "Who done that?" Silence. All five barracks, the entire company now, was subsiding. Like a turtle pulling its head in. Then, from Barracks 3 you'd hear, way in the distance, "*Buckabuckabuckabuckabuck!*"

"All right, you guys, I'm coming down there." It was the first sergeant. Then you'd hear him walking along the duckboards, *klunk, klunk, klunk, klunk*. He'd stop and he'd look in. "Smart guy!" Boom, he'd slam the door. To the next one.

Well, we sat, we sat. One week went by. Do you know the terrible torture of watching the entire camp going on a weekend leave? You could see them going past, the guys all dressed up, with their Dopp kits, their shaving kits, yelling and hollering. You saw the buses going. And, with red-rimmed eyes, we just stared out at the gray skies. And the snow was drifting down. Company K had bought it! Company K was getting it you know where. And you know what it was getting.

We just sat there and watched. The big thing of the week was the time we had eggs for breakfast one day. That became a tremendous, exciting thing. We rushed there on Sunday because they had eggs. Everybody ate eggs like mad and everybody went back and sat again. And watched.

How would you like it if the most exciting thing to happen to you in three weeks was to decide, finally, at long last after two years in the army you're going to do this? The only way you can get out of the company area was to go to chapel. Holy smokes! You never saw so many guys all of a sudden get religion. Just to get away from those crummy barracks. So everybody was sitting down there in chapel, and they had a rule that if your company was under detention, you had to go with one of the NCOs, to make sure you came back in a body. Imagine sitting in chapel and sitting behind you was the staff sergeant with his arms crossed, just watching. Nobody was going to make a break, boy, and there wasn't going to be any ad libbing in the hymns. We were all sitting there, and the only sound that we made was something like, "Bringing in the sheaves, bringing in the sheaves."

We sat and the snow kept drifting down. The chaplain got up and he gave a brief prayer, and then he gave the typical sermon that would be like, "Making the *best* of a difficult life." They always had that sermon in the army. "You realize that you are doing a great thing for humanity. And I want *all* of you to go back to your company area, men, I want all of you to look deep down inside of yourselves, realize the great opportunity you have, for not only serving your Creator, but you are also serving the people of the blessed United States," and all of us are saying, "…and that nut, Captain Cherry." That nut, too, Chaplain. Don't forget him.

One after the other we went immediately after chapel and we applied for our TS slips. That means going to the chaplain and telling him our trouble. And that chaplain would just sort of smile at you like a bowl of Jell-O. He just sat there, and he was a captain, so he had it made. He sat there with two chaplain assistants and they smiled like small bowls of Jell-O. All three of them sat there, and in the background someone would be practicing on the wind-driven organ. He'd say, "Now, son, just tell me what the trouble is."

"Well, I can't get out of the company area. I don't know what it is. I'm just sitting down in the barracks. I'm fed up with it, Chaplain!"

"Well, the ways of God and the army are sometimes difficult to understand, son."

Yeah, I know. You represent God and Cherry represents the army, and both of you are sitting with that smile on your face.

And you went back out into that cold company area with the snow drifting down gradually. Well, another week went by. Then it was two weeks and the guys were really out of their skulls. Oh boy! Talk about stir crazy. It was Monday, then Tuesday. Day after day dragging by like it was some ancient animal—with three legs. Wednesday, then Thursday and everyone was wondering—are we getting out of this, at last? This was inhuman. This treatment went beyond cruelty. It became nuttiness at that point. And sure enough, late Thursday night after a twenty-five-mile forced hike in the snow. Twenty-five miles, we came back.

We were now gaunt. Our ribs were sticking out through our fatigues, our battle jackets crusted with frost, our eyes glazed and angry, our fangs were long. And up ahead of us was the captain marching. We were coming back. Have you ever marched behind a nut? He was bobbing up and down ahead of you, his little tin hat going up and down. All your tin hats going up and down. The wind blowing through your ears, and you felt your rifle bobbing up and down on your back and your canteen and your mess kit and your gas mask slapping you. And up ahead was that fantastically *hateful* head. It looked like a bug or something and everybody looking at him, and he was up there, "Come on men, let's go! Let's show 'em we're the best damn outfit in the whole camp! Let's double-time into camp!"

Double-time into camp after twenty-five miles! That means run. That means putting on a big show the last minute. You run. We go *hup huh hup huh hup huh*, gasping, and everybody watching as we went galloping past. Company K was back from its bivouac. We came trotting past those silent barracks. Those were the happy companies, you see. Company M, Company N, The 3175th, all the happy outfits, the guys who looked clean-shaven, that were kind of fat, they had clean uniforms. All of us had high cheekbones, with red-rimmed eyes. We came trotting past and we got out in front of the company area.

He stopped us. "All right, you guys, at ease. At ease! Shut up, Gasser, at ease!" And he stands. First sergeant hollers, "Attent-*hut*! The guns rattle, everything rattles. The snow drifting down. Two hundred twenty-seven guys standing at attention. And a slow smile came over the captain's face. "Men, I have an announcement to make. Anybody that wants a weekend pass starting twelve-noon Saturday, apply down at the orderly room after retreat. Anybody wants a pass, apply at the orderly room. Any questions?"

We just don't want to breathe. You just don't want to break the magic spell. We're getting out, we're getting out this weekend. Oh boy! Holy smokes! And the wind is blowing and the snow is drifting down and the clouds are gray. We're hungry. We've been eating K rations for two days, we've been drinking chlorinated water out of our canteens. We can smell the mess hall down there cooking up a big batch of SOS. Everybody's getting all excited. Oh man! Don't say anything. Don't goof up, guys. Stand still! *Shhhhh!*

"Any questions?" Silence. "All right, dismissed!" *Boom*, we go like a gigantic explosion! We run into the barracks, yelling and hollering, and we sit down on our bunks and all of a sudden we love him! We love this nut. We love this insane nut. By the way, one of the secrets of the true tyrant—give 'em nothing for a hundred years and then you give 'em one small lump of sugar and they'll lick your boots for ten million miles, believe me. We loved this guy—"Ah, he was just kidding us for three weeks. Lemme tell you, boy. Boy, he sure shaped us up. Yeah, wow!" This is a fantastic moment of joy. Wonderful outflowing of it.

So we stand out there tall and straight for retreat and everybody's in his Class A uniform. For the first time you really feel great. You're seventeen feet tall and the flag goes up and everybody salutes and the cannon booms and we all split. We're all sitting in the mess hall eating the old SOS and the bread and drinking the coffee and the guys are all yelling and hollering and eating the Jell-O. It's funsville again, and you should have seen the crowd eat in about thirty seconds and pour out, and we're all lined up in front of the orderly room applying for the pass. The whole company, to a man, is out in front.

We arrive at the desk: "Give your name, rank, and serial number." "Shepherd, J. P., corporal, 16098946." "All right, pass, put your name down here. T5, right, right." One after the other we go down the line, every last guy.

Like Christmas time. It's like sleeping before Christmas. Everyone all excited. Friday night goes by on wings of song. You're knee-deep in the grease pit and you're singing "Noel." You're singing a happy birthday song. Boy, it's all wild and great.

Saturday morning dawns bright and clear and the captain is having barracks inspection. Can you imagine a guy coming into your pad every Saturday morning, a maniacal nut, and he's got another guy with him who carries white gloves. Coming in and looking under the daybed to see whether there's any dust. He goes under the radiator with his white gloves. Everybody's just standing there at attention by their bunks. Guts pulled in.

The captain sweeps down the middle of the barracks like Genghis Kahn and behind him is his first sergeant and the exec. They walk down the barracks dressed to the nines in their Class A uniforms and we've got ours on. They walk down, looking each man in the eye. "Serial number, rank?" He knew all of us very well. He's become very GI. "Give me the sixth general order, mac." And the guy bangs it out—*boom!* "Walk my post in an orderly manner." *Boom!* Boy, we're all really sharp. "Lemme see your piece there." Down comes the rifle. He holds it up to the light. Clean as a whistle. His eyes are blinded by the fantastic gleam. He slaps it in your gut. *Bang!*

"All right, at ease, men. No demerits in this barracks. Congratulations." *Ooooh!* Fantastic exhalation. He goes into the next barracks. You hear the silence. *Klump, klump, klump,* the little muffled talk, and then, finally, the screen door slam shut in the back, "No demerits in Barracks 2, Sergeant." *Ooooh!* Because we're all in this together. We know that if Barracks 3 louses up, we're dead just as much as if we did. We know it. Finally he gets down to Barracks 5 and we are in the clear! What a moment!

It's now twelve noon, and in fifteen minutes our passes become set. Suddenly that little thing there in the corner, that idiot thing, that squawk box, goes off. "This is the first sergeant. Before you fall out, the captain wants you to all fall out in your overcoats. Fall out in your overcoats, Class A uniforms in the company street. Fall out in five minutes. On the double. Fall out! You can pick up your pass after the formation, men."

Goonk! What's up? What's up? That sick feeling. What is it? What is it? What's up? What's up? Oh, well, he just wants to see if we've brushed our hair, ha, ha, that's all.

Everybody's pulling on his coat. The big overcoat we wear in the army. The snow is drifting down and it's beautiful, a beautiful day. Everybody's got his eyes on the big town, he's thinking of chicks, he's thinking of the USO. All the *big* stuff. He can hardly wait! And we all fall out, one after the other, and now the entire company is out there. Across the road, guys in those other barracks are already leaving. They've got their Dopp kits—we don't care, we're going! All dressed up. And then comes the whistle. "Attention!" We stand at attention. We're all dressed up just like in the movies and this is the first time for us, with our sharp, new hats on and our OD shirts and our ties. Our uniforms are buttoned and we are all wearing our overcoats and we're waiting to see what's going to happen.

The captain walks out of the orderly room. He's dressed magnificently. Have you ever seen an officer in full flower? When you're a GI, an officer's clothes look like they're made out of gold and silver. Even their pants look different. He comes walking out in front of us and looks at us. For maybe about a minute and a half. He nods to the sergeant. The sergeant says, "Attention! Attention, men!" With that the captain reaches into his greatcoat pocket and takes out a metal measuring tape. Everyone thinks, what's the nut going to do? What's this?

The snow is drifting down. It's a cold day. The temperature has maybe dropped twenty degrees in the last twenty-four hours and it's now about fifteen degrees. Cold puffs of a desolate wind are falling across our faces, freshly shaved, ready to go out on the swingers' town. He stands there quietly and then he pulls the tape out maybe an inch and a half and he goes down to the first platoon. What's this nut up to?! He goes up to the first man in the first platoon and stands next to him and begins to measure the distance between the top of the patch on his coat to the seam! What is that nut doing?! What is this? And one by one he takes each guy and says, "Pass cancelled." And one by one he takes each guy and says, "Pass cancelled."

Pass cancelled, we hear. *Ohhhhh!* The whole company takes one deep breath. There is a regulation that says your patch must measure one and a quarter inches exactly, from the top of the patch to the seam of your coat. It is very difficult to measure that—when you are sitting in the cold barracks—trying to sew it on yourself. Not only that, it is open to interpretation. Do you measure from the top of the seam or the bottom of the seam? Do you measure from the top of the rim of the patch or the bottom?

And the captain is making his own interpretation each time. Two hundred twenty-seven men and not a man has a one-and-a-quarter hiatus between the patch and the seam.

With that the captain turns, snaps his rule, puts it in his pocket, gets in his jeep, and drives towards the BOQ. The BOQ, by the way, is Oz—that's the Emerald City. That's where the rich guys live. That's like the boss, getting in his Cadillac and driving off to Park Avenue. "Stew in your own juice, fellows, you'll like the mailroom." And we stand there and turn, go back to the barracks. And there isn't a single sound.

Not a sound. Guys were taking their ties off. A guy way down the end started shining his shoes. And we saw, across the company street, the 3172nd and the 3173rd, those guys couldn't believe their eyes! They couldn't believe this! They have seen all kind of chicanery in the army, they have seen insults beyond insults, but they couldn't believe it. And they looked at us as though we were guilty. Obviously we deserved what we got. And you know, it's a funny thing, by about four o'clock in the afternoon, we were convinced that once again we had loused up. And by five o'clock already, we were repenting. And by six o'clock, when we were sitting there in the old mess hall eating pork and beans, we were beginning to yell at one another. "How come we let this get by?" "Why didn't we think of it?" "No wonder he did it to us!" "I don't blame him!" "I don't blame him for feeling the way he does about us!" "I don't blame him!"

T. S., MAC

I only went once to see the chaplain when I was in the army. Just once. And I went there when I was really bugged down. I was on my bunk, and everything was sneaking up. You know how things sneak up on you, you hear things in the weeds and you see little flickering flashes up there in the sky and the insufferable forces of life are beginning to creep up on you on a snake's belly. And finally, I was sitting there on the edge of the bunk and I had my head in my hands and I said, "Oh, darn," and I was yelling and hollering, "Oh boy, *blahblahblahblahblahblahblahblahblah*!"

And finally Gasser, down at the other end of the barracks, said, "Hey, Shep."

I said, "Yeah, whatta ya want?"

He said, "Why don't you go see the chaplain, mac?" In the army that's a putdown. Nobody really, seriously does. He said, "Ah, go see the chaplain!"

I said, "By George, I think I will. I think just maybe I will!"

So I dragged my you-know-what down along the company street, raising dust as I went. Yeah. I dragged it down that company street, past the orderly room, past the day room, and out into the crisp, cold, unfriendly sunshine of life. I wended my weary, unhappy way toward the chaplain's tent. Looking for solace, looking for sympathy, looking for just a smidgen of love. Looking for who-knows-what.

Ten minutes later I was admitted to the tent of the chaplain. There was this little, skinny kid up in the front there. I have never once seen a drama on television or in the movies about that type of soldier. You know the kind of soldier who plays the organ for the chaplain? Did you know there are guys like that? They have little rimless glasses and they have a very official, supercilious air as though they are in touch with the infinite. They have got a direct pipeline to G-O-D. And also to the chaplain. Which in many cases is synonymous.

They sit in the front of the tent and they're wearing their Pfc stripes, and everything is very pressed on these guys, and all the time they look very clean. Clean-scrubbed look. You know the scrubbed look of righteousness? You've seen that. We've all faced that, that look in the eye that looks right at you that says, "Well, it serves a sinner right!"

He had that look. He was God's little raindrop right here down on the earth with us. He was sitting there by his little folding GI OD-covered organ, admitting in the victims one by one to see the chaplain. He rejected other guys, too—if you came and he didn't like your looks and figured you were just a little too much of a sinner. A *rotten* sinner! He just sent you back to the company area, and maybe you'd pick up a few days of KP for your sins.

I was in line there—I don't know why I got started on this story of religious life in the army—I was there to see the chaplain. I figured if I saw the chaplain, I could wangle a three-day pass out of it.

I figured if I could get away from the area for a while, if I could split out of this camp I was in for about three days, and lay in a couple of beers and visit a few people I knew, and make a few judicious phone calls, and go to a few places that I knew about going to, maybe I'd come back with a spring in my step. Singing happy songs. Ready to go. But you can't quite tell the chaplain *that* story, see. So you have to come in dragging your you-know-what behind you, and with a little cloud of dust flying behind you, and that look of the man who is at the breaking point.

Well, I sit down in front of the chaplain. He also has a round, scrubbed face. He has that clear look, rimless glasses, he parts his hair in the middle, and sits there with the look of the man—I don't know how to express it—that look of the man—he is like the Pfc-in-the-front-by-the-organ—squared. And he sits there and looks at me for a long while and I'm telling him my story. And I'm playing it all the way, you know. I'm an old "method" sufferer. I suffer from inside, and, as a good sufferer, like a good Stanislavski actor, can reach hidden depths, he can dredge it out of his soul. I'm speaking, I'm crying: "I was sitting there, *waaaa*, mess hall... and I'm... *ahaaaa, ohhh, waaaa*." I'm talking away there, I'm just wringing it out, just feeling the scene. Any good actor can feel the scene. He knows when he's milking it. He can just feel it. The excitement. Because it begins to come out. And the tears are real, live, crocodile tears pouring down my suntanned cheeks, and my corporal stripes there are damp with the tears of humanity. I'm crying away. He's looking at me, and after a long pause, I go, "I *waaa... an... oh... ... yaoooooooo*!" And I finish my story.

He looks at me and he says, "Hum! Well, humph, well." (I don't know whether I can say what he says then. Remember, he is not only a chaplain, he is in the army. And there are certain army phrases. And this army phrase consists of two letters, the first one of which is a T.) He shrugs his shoulders and says, "Well, *blahabahaaa*." He looks past me and calls out, "Send the next one in, Charlie."

I stand up. I say, "Is that all?"

He says, "Heh. Humph. Yep."

And I see a sudden flicker in his eye. It's very, very—how should I put it? It is a moment of great revelation to me. A little flicker in his eye. That he is looking for a chaplain—to go tell *his* problems to. And once he gets to that chaplain, that chaplain would look at him with the same look in the eye of a man who is looking for a chaplain to tell his troubles to. It kind of goes to infinity. This little fat man with the little cross on his collar looks at me and says, "Heh, what're ya gonna do?"

I say, "Yes sir."

I salute, and he gives me a limp Presbyterian- slash-Methodist- slash-Baptist-slash-Roman-Catholic salute, and just a quiet "Huh."

I walked past that Pfc sitting there with his little folding organ at the front of the tent. He was sitting there with that snotty look of a guy who was in touch with the Ten Commandments he felt he had something to do with. Maybe, perhaps, he had co-authorship rights. And he was sitting looking up at me and I looked at him. A little, brief moment of looking, and then he said, "Want me to punch your card, mac?"

And I uttered one of the old, ageless army phrases that the yardbirds who followed Hannibal's elephants must have said from time to time.

He said, "Yeah?" And he looked back into the tent where another sufferer, another penitent, was sitting in front of the little round man with the rimless glasses, getting solace from man's ills.

Is there anybody out there who has had his card punched recently? I was once in a company, briefly, that actually issued cards. Literally. Somebody had a little printing press down in the supply room and he printed them up. And everybody in this company had a little card marked with those two famous letters, and little places for chaplains to inscribe on the back various indignities that are heaped on us. What ex-GIs can tell me what that card was known as—it's a general phrase.

PAYDAY

There are certain things in your life which attain a kind of curiously hallucinogenic quality. That have no real basis in reality. It's like, it's hard to remember a specific day from school. School is hallucinatory, almost a dream existence, because it's hard to grasp any particular moment. The army is even more than that.

I remember one night at Fort Monmouth, New Jersey. I've been in the army now for two years. When you've been in that long, it's your life. You don't think of being out. You don't think of any other existence other than the now. And one of the very few groovy things about being in the service is that you live for this instant—payday. You don't save your pay. In fact I have known of guys who have gotten rid of their pay in less than twelve milliseconds after it's handed to them. Why? Because it's only of the now—this instant! And so it is payday.

You know what it's like to be paid in the army? You never see this scene in army movies or marine movies—you never see them getting paid. You always see them in combat—which is a very tiny part of the whole world of the army. It's such a tiny part that very few guys ever even get involved in it.

I remember a payday at Fort Monmouth. It's raining, a hard, driving rain, but that didn't matter—it's payday, and the tradition in the army is that on payday you're always paid in the middle of the week and you get a half-day, so immediately after pay you're free—you get a pass, you can go. It's a great thing—half-day. So it is now eleven-thirty in the morning, I'm sitting in the barracks.

I have not been paid for three months. I have not been out of tents and barracks buildings for three months or better. Why? I have been redlined, which means that when you arrive at the point where you're about to get paid, the sergeant who is doing the paying looks up and says, "You're redlined." That means you don't get paid and something bad is going to happen to you. Like you're going to get shipped, and so they withhold your pay.

For three months I would go down to the PX and just *look* at Milky Way bars, just watch guys eat them. If you can imagine being without scratch of any kind—without pay—any kind of money at all for three months and you can't go out or do anything. It's like being in jail for three months. So here it is, payday, and I'm sitting on the edge of my bunk in my Class A's and across, on the next bunk, is Gasser. The two of us don't realize we're about to be partners in a total disaster—one never knows this, and I say this is just as well. Right now I'm so excited.

We're sitting there and in comes Zinsmeister. He looks down the barracks and says, "Did you hear the rumor?" Well, that word, rumor, is one of the most fiendish words in the entire lexicon of the service.

Immediately, Gasser says, "What rumor?"

"Did you hear about it? Did you hear what they're going to do with Company K?"

Gasser says, "Don't tell me we're shipping again! We haven't been paid for three months!" (Actually, there were several words that he put into that sentence which I have deleted due to the fact that there may be women and children who do not know these words. I do not wish to be the one to bring these words to them.)

Pregnant pause. Zinsmeister says, "Worse than that."

Gasser says, "What could be worse than that?"

"Wait. I ain't gonna be the one to tell ya."

Five minutes later, the bugle call for pay blows through the rain. What a beautiful sound! It echoes throughout the entire camp, drifting out, and all the GIs in all the barracks are instantly united. They are all charging down to their dayrooms, and we're standing outside lined up according to rank. But there is one group that stands in front of all of them regardless of their rank. Gets right in front and is universally hated in the army. I am one of those guys and so is Gasser—we both have the magic serial numbers.

The dayroom is like the company club room, with a pool table and a Ping-Pong table and a Coke machine that gives out nothing but warm Coke. When they pay they usually put a green felt covering on the Ping-Pong table. And behind the table sits the first sergeant and next to him on one side sits the staff sergeant, and on the other side is the company commander, who does not sully his hands by touching mere filthy lucre, he just sits there in his dress uniform.

In front of the first sergeant, who is about to pay, is a big, fat, iron strongbox with a lock on it, and next to it is a loaded 45-caliber automatic pistol. The box is filled with cabbage, d-e-a-u-x, dough, bucks, bread, baby, the money! It is in cash—bread. They don't pay you in checks in the army. He also has a list next to him of all the guys who are about to receive what they are about to receive. The list also tells why they are not to receive what they thought they were going to receive. That's the pay roster.

It's a tremendous moment—almost like a moment in an opera when Mephistopheles is about to arrive. It's a moment when all things are still for an instant. The moment before they pay. The moment of sheer poetry and beauty. It's the anticipation. As a matter of fact, there was an entire Greek philosophy built on *anticipation*, rather than realization. The Stoics believed that to contemplate a sizzling steak and refrain from indulging is the basic ecstasy, that to indulge is to sate and destroy the basic anticipatory ecstasy. You follow? The *idea* of getting paid, *about to be* getting paid, is more exciting than *being* paid. Have you noticed that no sooner do people get a raise than they want another one? Because it's the same old problem—the guy gets a raise and his foot still hurts, his chick still puts him down, his Ford still burns oil—he can't figure out why. So he begins to plot for next year's raise. The idea of *about to be* getting a raise is more important that *having* a raise. Because once you get a raise it's not a raise anymore, it's just your crummy old rotten pay. Anticipation is much greater than realization. Always has been, always will be.

So here we are, all poised. All of Company K is arrayed out there in its magnificent Class A uniforms wearing our raincoats. And I'm in front of the line. There's a silence in the dayroom, and then, Sergeant Kowalski steps from behind his desk and walks over to the door and looks out through the screen and says, "All right, you guys, let's go." He sits back down at his table.

For those of you who have never seen an army pay, you have missed one of the most beautiful sights of this panoply and ritual. Everything is ritual in the army. There's a routine you follow when you get paid. You don't just come up and say, "Give me my money." You walk up to the table in a smart, military manner the way it's prescribed. You quickly pivot, you salute, and you say, "Shepherd, J. P., T/5, 1609846, reporting for pay, sir."

There is a pregnant pause.

First Sergeant Kowalski looks up and down the list, he turns to the company commander and says, "Twelve dollars and forty-seven cents."

The company commander looks at his list and says, "Twelve dollars and forty-seven cents, Sergeant."

The sergeant says, "Twelve dollars and forty-seven cents."

And then you say, "Excuse me, sir. May I ask a question?"

"What is it?"

"How come I've only got twelve dollars and forty-seven cents, sir?"

"You get all the dope at the orderly room after pay. Here's your twelve forty-seven, move on." And he hands you the twelve dollars and forty-seven cents in bills and in small change. At which point you salute, pivot smartly, and you go back out into the rain. And everybody else goes through the same routine.

And then, at that moment, the moment of release, Gasser and myself got on a bus with our twelve dollars and forty-seven cents. The first bus that came along in front of that camp. We didn't even know where it was going. The first one that came. We had to get out.

It was still kind of rainy, getting darker. We sat on that bus. There were only three of us in the bus and we went to a town which I have never heard of before or since, Keansburg, New Jersey. With our twelve dollars and forty-seven cents, me and Gasser fled through the screaming, howling night to Keansburg, New Jersey, in search of ecstasy, truth, and beauty.

I remember the bus stopping on the main street of Keansburg next to a chili joint. Gasser and I got out and it was raining like Billy-be-damned. It was coming down.

Gasser said, "What'll we do?" He was all excited.

I said, "How about some chili?"

Gasser said, "Yeah. Let's have some chili."

That's what you do in the army. We went in and had four bowls of chili, six beers, went out in back and threw up, and continued to walk down the street looking for more ecstasy. We found a little boardwalk. We walked around the merry-go-round twelve times. Five hundred, a thousand times, me and Gasser walked around the merry-go-round in the rain, enjoying the magnificent ecstatic night in Keansburg, New Jersey.

People kept going up and down on these wooden horses—that is, about six or seven other GIs from Company M kept going up and down on the wooden horses. Then we walked back down through the rain and got on the eleven-ten bus. The only bus that left Keansburg, New Jersey. And headed back to Fort Monmouth. I had sixty-six, maybe sixty-seven cents left after that night of wild debauchery in Keansburg eating chili, drinking beer, riding up and down on a wooden horse, and throwing balls at kewpie dolls. I'll never forget Keansburg, New Jersey. It represents the *Carnivale*.

POWs

The war was going full tilt, and one day they brought in this bunch of raggle-taggle Italian prisoners. The first thing that knocked us out about them was they were all about a foot and a half shorter than we were. It seemed like they had raided all the elves and brought this whole bunch of them. It must have been two or three battalions of little guys they'd gotten from somewhere. We were fascinated by them. They had these strange-colored uniforms, uniforms that looked like they had been left out in the rain too long and that looked like they had been another color before. For some reason or another it was very difficult to get mad at them. They were just sort of walking along, must have been about a hundred and fifty of them in a bunch, sort of shuffling in, and they put them into barracks.

About three days later, it was the damndest thing you ever saw in your life. Remember, this was a GI camp—very GI, with square corners, nothing but gravel and little ditches by the side of the road and everything trampled down. Not one bit of décor except maybe a flag somewhere. All the Italians had come out of their barracks, and with some whitewash they had gotten somewhere, they had taken all the rocks they could find and had painted them white. They built little fences around their barracks out of the white stones and then they built rock gardens with hearts and flowers and little Madonnas all put together out of rocks. It was right out of New Jersey, with stone deer and rubber Mexicans in front of the houses, all there in front of the barracks.

It was a very odd thing that this did to us. You see, we were being trained to be tough, and we were very hard-bitten-type guys, and suddenly we saw these guys who had just been brought in from North Africa with their little hearts and flowers in front of their barracks. It was very demoralizing, and once in a while somebody would try to get mad.

The prisoners had been given strange uniforms with orange bands around their arms so you could recognize them. Of course you could identify the Italians from a mile away because they didn't walk like soldiers or anything. They were allowed to just walk all around just like the rest of us GIs. You went to the PX and there they'd be. About a hundred and fifty GIs—great big hunks from the Midwest, scratching and hollering—and scurrying around would be about seventeen or eighteen little Italian GIs with their orange bands on them. They must have been given Red Cross packages or something, because they had little certificates that they could trade in for Milky Way bars.

These Italians were in there trading for Milky Way bars and nobody knew quite how to feel, because, after all, they were the enemy—and they're fooling around in the PX. These little guys, weighing a hundred and five pounds and standing there real sad. What are you going to do, holler at them, "Enemies!" and hit one in the face?

Apparently, among Italians all over Jersey, the word got out that there were some Italian prisoners in this camp. Because every Sunday there would be forty-five thousand Italians outside the gate all along the fence, and all the Italian GIs would be lined up inside looking out. You'd hear them yelling back and forth. You never saw more Italian chicks from Jersey in your life, standing outside the gates talking to the Italian GIs. Obviously they didn't know them—they were just Italian. They were handing stuff to them, bread and so on.

Apparently somebody had smuggled in ninety-four thousand pounds of geranium seeds, because within weeks you saw, around the front of the prisoners' barracks, along with the white hearts and flowers and little Madonnas, there were geraniums growing. And all night long you could hear them hollering and singing. I must say that from those days on, I formed a *great* and lasting, abiding affection for the Italians. Which is very difficult to explain.

A PLACE OF REST AND COMFORT

I have a five-day pass and I'm kind of broke. I go down to the train station in Washington, which looks exactly the same today as it always did. And I'm kind of tense because I want to get home and I had just gotten this pass. I had not had a pass in months and a lot of things are happening in my life and it is a very cold, cold, cold night.

I have my ticket and they were supposed to have reserved seats on this train. But right from the start the entire system of the trains and everything else has broken down. So this crowd of people is already *on* the train. That's what always seems to happen to me. It's a strange phenomenon. Anyway, I go struggling into this train with a lot of other victims and they're all sitting there, fat, dumb, and happy. They look like they've been here for two weeks, they have all kinds of stuff spread out, they're reading, their kids are crying. The place is packed, so I decide to walk all the way to the end on the platform. I figure if I go down to the end, I would get where the empty cars are. Well, that is a tactical error. Apparently the train had filled up from that other end first, because by the time I get near that end, each car I walk by is filled more than the one behind it, and I see other people behind me going into places where I'd already said, "Well, there's no room there." So, even before I get on the train it's like a toothpaste tube that has not yet been opened. It is packed, man, and I mean packed! So packed that people are standing in the aisles.

I say to the conductor when I get on, "You know, I have my ticket. I'm supposed to have a seat."

He says, "All right, come on, buddy, don't block the aisles. We gotta get through." No way he is going to help. He has the blue hat, the big, billowy coat on, the watch with the chain, and all that stuff.

So I'm standing in the aisle with the crowd. I figure that what was going to happen was that a lot people were going to get off in Baltimore. I figure I'd stand up until Baltimore, which is only a short way, but it is so hot on the train, you couldn't believe it. If they had tapped this train with a pipe it probably could have heated the city of Chester, Pennsylvania, just from the extra heat. Oh, my God, it's about a hundred and fifteen degrees. And kids are crying. And I'm standing up.

At first you feel hopeful that it would cool down and you'd get a seat. I look around but I don't know a soul. There are a few sailors, a couple of other GIs, and some guys wearing exotic uniforms. And the crowd is just packed. Finally the train starts to roll and I'm swaying there with my little bit of luggage. All I have is a Dopp bag with my toiletries and a flight bag. Nothing to sit on. Finally I ask this old lady sitting there, "Can I sit on the edge of your armrest, madam?"

She says, "What was that?"

"Can I sit on the armrest for a minute?"

She says, "If you do I'll call the conductor. This is *my* seat!"

Oh, for God's sakes! "Be nice to the boys in uniform," they say. So I say, "Thank you very much, lady."

"Don't be sarcastic to *me*!"

I say, "Don't be sarcastic to *me*!"

"I'll call the conductor!"

The train has just started, we were out of the station for maybe thirty seconds, and already I'm tangling with this old doll. I say, "Excuse me, lady."

"Don't bother me."

I struggle down the car length. I want to get away from that nut. I struggle down maybe fifteen or sixteen seats further, fighting my way through guys who are sitting in the aisle on the floor, others sitting on suitcases. Finally I can't go any further because of a knot of guys. Have you ever seen people *standing up* playing pinochle? But that's what they are doing, and you don't walk through a pinochle game. So I stand there for a while. The train is rolling on and, of course, I can hardly wait till we get to Baltimore.

We're just rolling and it's getting hotter and hotter and hotter and hotter and kids are crying more and more and finally, after it seems maybe two or three weeks the train starts going *ding ding ding ding ding ding*, you know how it does that sound, and it goes into a tunnel *ding ding ding ding ding*. Suddenly daylight and flashing by the window is a sign that says Baltimore. Oh great! Great! Finally, oh boy! Just when my knees are starting to give out. *Ding ding ding ding ding* and we stop.

I can't believe my eyes! Out on the platform must be five thousand other people. The doors open and in they come! Nobody goes! This is something else! How can they do this? And sure enough, they're doing it, packing them in, and there's a couple of conductors running around on the outside, and they have these big rug-beaters to drive people in, and they're packing them in. "Get in there! Move! We've gotta get goin'!" So they pack the crowd in and finally we get the last victim packed in. The train is buttoned up. This train is as filled as a football full of air. Just packed.

And we start to roll. It's getting dark, and this train, by the way, had been billed as a "dinner train." A "dinner train." What a joke. So there's a "dining car." That car was filled from the moment we took off in Washington, all the way to Chicago, apparently by none of the passengers. There's a crowd of well-dressed, elegant people who keep drinking wine. I know none of the rest of us got in there. And we're rolling through the night.

And I'm standing there dressed in my full, Class A wool uniform. After all, it's winter. And I had made an unbelievable mistake. I really made a mistake. Usually, when you dress in Class A uniform, you wear a suntan shirt under your wool uniform. Well, I figured that for a little touch of exotic elegance, I would wear my OD, which is my dark wool shirt under my uniform. An interesting, exotic variation of the uniform and totally legal, but it has its dangers. I had on the shirt, for starters, very good, top-flight wool, tightly woven. In fact it's a special shirt that you're issued that has been treated so that it's gas-resistant, so gas doesn't seep in and burn your skin if you're gassed. I can only say that next to a New York Jets rubber sweatshirt, this shirt is the most effective garment that I know of for generating internal heat and external sweat. I'm sweating like crazy and it's pouring off me in rivulets. The shirt, the wool pants on, and what the army calls a blouse, a dress coat with brass buttons, all soaked through with sweat.

I'm crouched down and I'm halfway to the floor with my knees up and for the first time I can see the floor, which is indescribably filthy! Candy bars from the time of the Second Battle of Bull Run, cigar butts, bottle caps, all this stuff rolling around on the floor. If you've ever been in a train that's packed, you know how rarely they clean these cars. I'm getting more and more depressed. And I don't know what time it is because my watch has stopped. It seems like we're going forever and it's getting even hotter.

At that point I say, the hell with it. You wear a tie when you're traveling in the army, but I take it off and stick it in my blouse, and I open the top two buttons of my shirt, and I'm scrunched down there still sweating. I'm starting to get a cramp that's hitting me in the back of the thighs so I stand up very painfully. Here's these guys playing pinochle in front of me and people crowded behind me and another guy drinking out of a bottle, and the kids are crying and the sweat's pouring down.

I hear this voice that says, "All right, soldier, what's your name? Give me your name and I want to see your pass."

I turn. Two MPs. What they're nailing me for in the middle of all this is "No tie," for God's sake!

I say, "Come on, gee whiz, wow, it's a hundred forty-eight degrees!"

"We only carry out the orders, bud, we don't make 'em. You're in train-travel, you've got Class A uniform on, so you wear your tie, and you ain't got no tie on, buddy. Name, rank, gimme your pass and I want to know what your outfit is."

"Company K, 362nd..."

"I want the real outfit."

"Here it is. Here's my dog tags." I yank my dog tags out and he writes down my serial number.

I'm getting gigged on my pass in the middle of this heat! But these MPs look sharp. I don't know how they do it. White helmet, white lanyards all over, big white holster. He says, "Okay, buddy, on with the tie. We'll be back in half an hour and if you ain't got that tie on, buddy, you're gonna be in real trouble, okay?"

I say, "All right, Sergeant," with just a tiny touch of sarcasm.

"Now look, don't give me any lip."

"Yes, Sergeant."

They go struggling off into the crowd. Gigged! Well, we roll on and on, hour after hour. The conductor calls out "Cumberland, Maryland." We're rolling through Cumberland Pass, nothing but blackness outside of those grimy windows. By this time they have turned the lights down somewhat. All these people in all these seats and piled up one on top of the other are now lying there with their mouths hanging open snoring, sleeping away, and there's the crowd of victims in the aisles who do not have seats. Guys were falling asleep standing up, but I have never been able to do that.

I'm swaying back and forth and my head goes out into left field and I'm getting kind of curious delusions or something and its getting hotter and hotter again. I figure I gotta get out of this. I'm gonna go crazy! I can see the headlines: "Soldier runs berserk in train. Slays seven with sharpened dog tags!"

I'm swaying in this car and I'm saying, "I gotta go, I gotta go!" I start struggling toward the rear of the train. I figure, if I can get toward the back, all the way to the back. I struggle through the mob blocking my car and now I'm between cars. There's five people jammed into this place between cars and you can see the tracks going by underneath, *KAGUNGA-GUNGA-GUNGA*, rolling, hot air blowing from the car and cold air blowing from outside and cinders and crud flying up out of the darkness.

I struggle my way and the next car is worse than the others. It's really jam-packed and has a strange smell like four drunks had drunk gallons of cheap wine and thrown up in the aisle and I gotta get through this car. I'm just delirious.

I see a dim crossing go by out in the darkness and I see a gas station sitting there dimly lit and I see gates come down and a car waiting for us to pass. I don't know where we are, what place we are in, what state, what nation, what country. It could be the River Styx. I have the feeling that I have died. I am in Hell. Nothing could be like this.

I struggle and I arrive at a car that says NO ADMITTANCE. To hell with no admittance, so I push the door open and I go in. It's a car that railroad men use, with racks all over the walls and tools and pipes hanging and big cables hanging down and it's dimly lit by a single yellow light bulb hanging down in a metal cage from the ceiling and it's swaying back and forth. This is the only car on the train that is cool. And I see sitting under the light bulb four guys with train caps and overalls. One guy with a conductor's cap turns when I come in and his back is to me. He looks around and says, "You can't be in here, buddy. You're not supposed to be here."

I say, "I just got to have a breath of air. Can I just stay for a minute to get my breath? I gotta get some air."

"Well, I'll tell you what you do. You see that little latch on the bottom of that door? Push it to your right. I don't want nobody else coming in here. You can stay a couple of minutes."

I turn and lock the door and I'm standing in the dim car there. For the first time I'm relatively comfortable and I've been on this train ten or fifteen hours—it is hard to say how long because my head is going off and I am delirious half the time. I've got my Dopp bag and my little flight bag and the sweat is starting to get cold now because it's cool in here. I see that there are boxes all piled up in this car. All kinds of crates. And these guys are playing cards on one.

I say, "Excuse me, conductor, can I sit on one of these crates back here? Can I sit down?"

He says, "Yeah, go ahead. Don't worry about it." He says, "Hey, Steve, is it okay?"

And Steve, who looks like an official type says, "Go ahead, go on, kid, take it easy. Just don't open that door back there. You can rest back here."

So I sink down on a big, long case and these guys are paying no attention, playing cards. I'm sitting on the case and I'm tired. I'd been out on bivouac and I'd had about two hours sleep in the last seventy-two and now I've been riding this train and I'm hot and I haven't had anything to eat and I'm going out of my mind and the sweat is rolling down into my socks. So I start to fall asleep sitting on this case, just swaying through the night. These guys are playing cards. I pull my feet up and stretch out full length on the case. We're riding along and I keep waking up as we stop at a siding.

And all of a sudden I'm awake and guys are shaking me. "Let's go, buddy. What are you doing here?" And I see the whole side of the car is open and we've pulled up to a siding. It is just barely dawn and I realize what I've been sleeping on. It's a coffin. I see some people outside on the tracks there waiting for this coffin. The five guys in the train grab hold of it and move it to the open side of the car and they put a folded flag on top of it. It's a GI. It's one of my buddies.

And I see the people outside take this coffin. And the doors close. And we start rolling again.

SEPARATION CENTER

One day they announced on the bulletin board that the following men were eligible for separation. Well, we all had been eligible for separation since the third or fourth year of the Boer War. I was eligible before I got in, actually. There were the names on the board. We couldn't believe it. We went back and sat down, and Edwards, of course, playing it cool, said, "I'll get my stuff packed. I'll be ready," and he started to pack. Abernathy was asleep so he missed the one formation he shouldn't have missed. I think he's still in the army.

We all marched off. They took us to the train and they let us off at Fort Dix, New Jersey. It was cold the December day we got there and the wind was blowing great gusts of snow.

At that time, they had working there various POWs. There were German SS men on KP. And I saw an incident. I saw a guy, a real grizzled GI, scuffling along ahead of me who looked like he'd been in the army five years. We came to the chow line and we were all standing there, working our way up. Like the Horn & Hardart, the guy saying "What'll you have?" And standing there serving, there was this POW who was about six feet four inches tall, blond, the very picture of the Hitler Jugend—the whole thing. Remember, we were also Jugend. We were all about nineteen or twenty. This guy ahead of me—you could see he was much older than the rest of us. Nobody talked to him—we were in a separation center, so nobody knew anybody, just our little knot of guys going through together.

All of a sudden, ahead of us, the guy had his big tray where KPs were throwing food into the little partitions. He took his tray—the only time I've ever seen it done—this POW gave a big scoop of SOS, he laid it down there and he was going about his business, and the GI said, "Hey, you, *achtung*!" and the POW turned around, and with that, the yardbird took his tray and—right in the face, just like that—*Pow*!

There was a kind of a dead silence and the POW sort of backed away, he had SOS and mashed potatoes falling down all over him, gravy all over his blond crew cut. He sort of backed away, looked with those cold blue eyes. The yardbird who hit him with the tray turned around and said, "Master race! I'll master-race you!"

And we went through the chow line. A very strange moment. You don't hear about these stories like this. I went drifting out into the company area—it was cold and bitter—little realizing I was about to have one of the great educational moments of my life.

There was a strange atmosphere in the camp. Very peculiar. You see, the entire place was filled with a very special kind of guy who had just come back. There were about ten elements of the 82nd Airborne that had just returned. And boy, they were something, I can tell you that! And there were about six thousand guys who had been in the 101st Airborne. And now these guys were back home and they began to resent all of their life that had gone. Guys weren't bugged at things that had happened in the army. All of a sudden it had become obvious that they had lost four years of their life! Just gone! Clipped right out! I remember looking out through these chicken wire fences at life beyond the army post. We could see all these guys walking around—civilian types—oh, they were very official and they were on top of it. Obviously they had been there and gotten somewhere. Radios were playing and you could hear all kinds of guys who had made it while you were gone. So all kinds of people who had lost those years were bugged.

About ten minutes after the mess incident, I was walking out in the wind and cold and darkness with Zinsmeister and Gasser, and we heard a lot of yelling. I saw that four GIs had two POWs trapped on the roof of a barracks. And it was snowing a terrible, icy snow, and these guys were throwing ice at them. These two Africa Corps POWs sitting up there, both kind of crouching down. You could see they didn't know which way to turn. A couple of MPs came along: "Come on, you guys, break it up, break it up."

We went wandering back to the barracks. So now we were sitting there. What were we going to do? Everybody had a sense of being at loose ends. There was no first sergeant any more, our lieutenant was shipped away and our captain was gone. The whole thing was all falling apart. Just beginning to disappear before your eyes.

While we were sitting there we listened to airplanes coming in to Fort Dix's airfield. A tremendous flight of B17s came in— big super-fortresses. They had just—*rghrammmmmmmmgh*! You just hear them one after the other, just come in from overseas, a squadron returning them *rghrammmmmmmgh*! And we watched them circle the field and lay them down one after the other out there in the darkness and you saw the lights blinking. And you could hear the POWs out in the street. That was the eerie thing about it. You could hear all these German voices all around out in the darkness. These guys were cleaning the streets and sweeping the sidewalks and you could hear them talking as we were all sitting there. Once in a while another airplane would come in *gwaaarghrammmmmmmm*! The walls would jiggle.

We sat there for four whole days with absolutely nothing to do. And these planes kept roaring in, and in came a glider group, a division that had been badly cut up in the jump over the Rhine *ghrammmmmmm*! It was the 17th Glider. They came roaring in and one of the planes crash landed coming in *bhawaurrrr*! And the smoke flying up. We just looked on. Nobody said anything. And all the while you could hear these German voices all around.

And *Yank Magazine* all of a sudden had no relationship to our own world anymore. Once in a while you'd see a guy walking around carrying something like the *Saturday Evening Post* or the *Daily News*. We heard newscasts on with guys saying, "Looks like the Yankees once again are going to…." All suddenly drifting back again. A peculiar resentment began to build up. Very strange kind of disorientation. Must be vaguely like—oh—some kind of reaction to an extended hospital stay when you've come through a peculiar kind of nightmarish, strange, involuted, delirious time, and suddenly you're back in it! You can't quite make—you resent people who are well. You're bugged at all these guys who are going to ball games and everything. Everybody was kind of milling around and Zinsmeister said, "Let's go down to the PX."

I was about to have an experience which I will never forget. So me and Gasser and Edwards and Zinsmeister went down to the PX. The PX in the separation center was very different from any other PX that I ever saw. Oh, they had wild stuff, like you could buy checkered tattersall vests—made out of Kleenex. Some of the stuff I wish I had bought now. I wish now that I had a pillow—this big red, white, and blue pillow that said, SOUVENIR OF FORT DIX SEPARATION CENTER. I would love to have that. I'd like to have that hanging in my office, with the gold fringe all over the thing.

So we were hanging around, we had our Milky Ways, we drank a couple of bottles of that GI beer. Really, GI beer made water look angry. On top of that I had a milkshake. You know, you go through those periods when you're just at loose ends—great phrase, you know. So, I had a milkshake and a couple of bottles of beer and then I had a cheeseburger and a Milky Way and then fooling around a little bit and Zinsmeister was eating stuff and Gasser was eating stuff and somebody said, "Let's get some Baby Ruths to take back" so we went over and bought a couple of Baby Ruth bars and I ate half of one and went back up again and had a tuna sandwich—you got nothing to do you just eat and scoff away.

And all this time the German POWs were walking around and making the scene with the chicks. Something about the Africa Corps really got to the chicks. We were just GIs, you know—they were exotic. And that bugged a couple of guys—"Hey, *heinie*, hey, hey. Get away from that chick, *heinie*." And the girl gave him a dirty look and the German didn't know what he was saying, he just sort of backed away. He could tell that look of the angry mortar platoon Pfc. There's a certain look. And so it just went on and on.

And then Zinsmeister, who was the man in our little group—he was grown up. He had a wife and all that stuff. All the rest of us, we were just—we were always asking, "Zinsmeister, how does it feel to be married?" He'd say, "Eh, you know…" He was the guy who experienced everything. We were just living alone.

And so Zinsmeister walked up to the counter and he said, "I'll have a half a dozen of those White Owls," and he got a half a dozen big, fat, cigars, the type that comes with a shoulder holster and it's got climbing irons on it. You know the kind—big, fat, obscene-looking cigar, really tough-looking cigar. Big band around it and that big owl looking out. So Zinsmeister came back and he had a handful of them and he passed them around. "Here, have a cigar, Gasser," and Gasser said, "No, I never smoke," and he said, "Here, Shep, have a cigar."

So I said, "Yeah, I'll have a cigar." I never smoked in my life! Maybe two cigarettes in all of my life I ever smoked. But we were getting out! It was all a celebration! The whole bit! You know, you're always drawn into these things. So Zinsmeister lit up, looking very—"Ahhhhh, Oh boy!" You know that thing—they roll them up a little bit and roll them around in their mouth and they take a match and hold it about a half inch below the cigar and it flares up and that purple smoke drifts around. And so I said, "Okay, got any matches, Carl?" He said, "Yeah."

I couldn't light it. I was puffing away and it wouldn't light.

He said, "Bite the end off."

So I said, "Oh, you gotta bite the end off?" So I bit the end off this thing and *whoooo*! Boy, the smoke came through, oh boy! It clears your sinuses and everything. Just like that. Your eyeballs start to water.

There must have been five hundred GIs all sitting around living the life of Riley and they were all smoking cigars and they had ruptured ducks, the whole bit, you know, they were all on their way out. And the Germans were walking around and once in a while someone yelled, "Hey, heinie! Beer! *Ein beer, ein beer, mach schnell.*" That was a typical expression, "*Mach schnell, heinie, ein beer.*" And the poor waiter would come over, who'd probably been a first lieutenant in some fantastic outfit, would lay the beer down and the guy would put his foot out and get him right in the tailbone and say, "*Mach schnell,*" and kick him. "Beer all around, heinie, *ach du lieber, Augustin.*"

Well, I started to puff that cigar. I must have puffed about three solid puffs, when I became aware that the PX was rising in the air! Just like that, it was beginning slowly to go up in the air! And I had a choking sensation. I had to get out, absolutely had to get out into the fresh air or I'd go….Ever had that feeling where you've gotta get out, gotta get out? The sweat was popping out and I felt this thing coming up from deep inside. It was like four years of gut-sickness coming up all at once. The whole thing. The excitement of getting out, the whole business, and I ran to the front door. There I am, the crowd of GIs coming, there's a crowd going out, the *heinies* are all over, and I run out. I'll tell you, I laid stuff all over the company area, stuff that I—frankly, there was a little piece of birthday cake that came up from my seventh birthday! It was fantastic! Little egg on it, it's the seventh! Holy smokes!

That night I went back to the sack and I lay down and the entire camp revolved around me with the B17s coming in and the *heinies* walking around and I could hear the GIs—"*Heinie, mach schnell, heinie.*" I'd hear the sound of a fist crunching—an 82nd Airborne was hitting a corporal in the mouth. Ohhhhh, what a night.

PART FIVE

MUSTERED OUT AT LAST!

Camp Murphy opened in 1942 and shut down operations in November 1944. Right before that camp closed, Shepherd attends the Army Specialized Training Program at the University of Maryland. Soon after Camp Murphy closes, T/5 Shepherd is sent to the Fort Dix Separation Center, where he encounters German POWs. He also recounts seeing Italian POWs at Fort Monmouth, New Jersey. He is discharged closer to home at Camp Atterbury, Indiana, on December 16, 1944.

The above chronology is based on documentary evidence; some of it is probably true, based on circumstantial evidence; some of it may be true because Shepherd says it is and there is no particular reason for him to have contrived it.

Some people look back on unpleasant experiences with nostalgia, but not Shepherd. He knows better. Enmeshed in the service or well out of it, Shepherd knows people are very much the same wherever they are. Some people refer to Shepherd as a humorist. He refers to himself as a realist.

When Jean Shepherd was discharged from the army in late 1944, his family, like most others, wanted to help him become reaccustomed to civilian life. Of course, the assumption is that military life is full of unpleasant, uncivil customs, brought on by the crude, rough-and-tumble ambiance of indentured servitude. Who knew what it had been like in the army, and who knew what might be necessary to turn the former soldier around to polite society?

The following episode, because of the understandings and misunderstandings regarding civilian and military life, warrants inclusion here. The meaning of the tale is a fitting conclusion to Shepherd's military bildungsroman, his "army novel." The core of the parable follows.

Discharged and back home in the civilized and conservative Midwest of Hammond, Indiana, Shepherd is maneuvered into a date with a minister's daughter, apparently to help him adjust to life away from the crudities of the military. Surely, this would provide an example of nice, normal, civilized life. She takes him to a wild honky-tonk bar, where she is obviously a regular customer. That she gets falling-down drunk seems evidence, as Shepherd frequently points out in stories and commentaries throughout his radio career, that no matter who you are and where you are, the essence of human behavior remains a constant.

Shepherd's experience of military life, as he told it and wrote about it, was a reflection of life everywhere, ironically made more intense and producing more open expression by both the rigid constraints and yet the anonymity of the system. The constraints sometimes led to a bursting of bounds where one found outlet. And the homogeneity of physical appearance of the uniform and the indistinguishable responses required by the system gave one the feeling of anonymity.

Shepherd sometimes told parables of two cavemen, Og and Charlie, in which he suggests that to this day, humans have not yet evolved into the rational, intelligent, lovely civilized people we think we are. Ol' Shep is well aware of the truth expressed in this witticism: They've finally found the missing link between primitive animals and civilized man—it's us.

Despite the military's best efforts to control humans, in even the best organized packs, Og and Charlie manage to find some free reign for their essence as the "missing link." In these always entertaining and frequently funny army stories, Jean Shepherd tells us something rather unsettling about ourselves.

One of the less pleasant experiences in the army is standing guard duty. Especially if it's winter, raining, and Christmas. In this final story, Shepherd thinks back on one such experience. Whatever he feels, it is not nostalgia.

—EB

THANK GOD I AIN'T IN THE ARMY!

"Guess who's picking up guard duty tonight at eight?"

I say, "Guard duty!"

"You bet."

Guard duty. I went back and I lay on my bunk and at ten minutes to eight I got up, slowly, got dressed, put on my raincoat, put on my gas mask, picked up my M-1, put on my cartridge belt, put on my leggings, put on everything that I had to put on including my tin hat, and I dragged myself down to the orderly room. And all the rest of that night I stood guard down at the end of the rifle range with the rain coming down and the wind howling around the shacks, moving back and forth, back and forth, my mind a total blank.

Once in a great while I would be reminded that it's Christmas. Off in the distance I'd see some GI walking along and I'd say, "It's Christmas!" And the wind would blow. And every half-hour a jeep would come around the corner, the rain slanting through the headlights. And the corporal of the guard would be sitting in the front seat. Once in a while with the officer of the guard.

And I remember the last go-round, my last trick was at six o'clock in the morning. Two-hour trick. And the guy came around, and he drove off in the mud, and as he drove off in the mud, he said, "Look," he said, "take it easy, soldja. Oh, by the way, Merry Christmas."

I said, "Merry Christmas, sir." I could see the glint of his wet first lieutenant's bars on his wet raincoat, and I had the vague feeling he didn't like it any more than I did. And somewhere, someplace, he too is probably saying, "It's Christmas Eve. Thank God I ain't in the army!"

APPENDIX

VERY ABBREVIATED ARMY GLOSSARY

Would you like to know some of the phraseology that is used in actual army conversation? You must be over twenty-one and a genuine, qualified student of psychology and sociology. Send your name and address to: "Cold Cuts." We will send you your list of absolute, authentic, GI expressions. Try them on your family and get ready to run.

—*Jean Shepherd*

Through exhaustive research of the Internet and requests to a vast, worldwide network of Jean Shepherd enthusiasts, only a couple of definitions worthy of view were encountered. Either upon release from service all former GIs surveyed were sworn to secrecy, or rusty brainpans were too unserviceable to assist. Nevertheless, a few amusing results can be sampled here (though none rising to the depths of obscenity Shepherd hinted at). But, as our story-telling master would put it at this point, women and children might well choose to blinder their peepers.

A FEW GENERAL TERMS

Cheesedick............................a brown-noser

Fart sack ....sleeping bag

Pecker checker..................... medical personnel

Pump and dunk................. urinate and defecate

Rectal cranial inversion. .to have one's head up one's ass

FOOD-RELATED VERNACULAR

Probably the army's best-known food term is SOS (creamed chipped beef on toast). "A culinary dish comprising a white sauce and rehydrated slivers of dried beef, served on toasted bread," as one source defines it. In the service it is universally defined as "Shit On a Shingle." Some civilians actually claim to enjoy it. Ugh!

Battery acid......................................coffee

Bug juice or
Purple Death ....Kool-Aid or other powdered drink

Cackleberry .... egg

KP
(kitchen
police) ....enlisted men assigned to mess hall drudgery

Moo juice .... milk

Mystery meat............ meat that lacks clear identity

Repeaters ......beans, sausage and other gas producers

Tube steak................................. hot dog

Jean Shepherd, in his days on the radio, could not say some words and expressions that come naturally to the naughty, Anglo-

Saxon tongues of most of us. As David Hinckley, Shepherd enthusiast and entertainment columnist for the *New York Daily News* put it, "Jean Shepherd knew all the four-letter words. If he could have used them on the radio, maybe he would have. But since he couldn't, he rendered them unnecessary." What Shepherd does is humorously suggest and play with the unmentionable, so that rather than regret the loss, we're provoked to laughter at his sly circumlocutions.

T. S., mac, which every kid as well as every soldier knows means, "Tough shit, mac." In polite society, the phrase becomes, "Tough stuff, mac," but soldiers, especially yardbirds, are not polite.

TRANSCRIBING SHEPHERD

On a discussion program after his radio days, a listener suggested that his radio stories merely needed to be transcribed from the audios of his shows to be converted into viable literature on the page. Shepherd responded, "Have you ever seen a tape transcribed? Well, come on now." He explained that it had taken him over a decade to get the feeling in his professional writing of a person talking. So, did he merely transcribe his spoken stories into the printed form? He said, "This is the last thing you can do." Shepherd knew he had to work on his transcripts—the stories in this book have been gently edited to the minimum possible. No new material has been added to Shepherd's works.

One of the pleasures of listening to Shepherd tell a story on the air is hearing the expressive variations in his voice and his skill in using his voice to create sound effects. "Fourth of July in the Army" is a good example, in which he makes vocal sound effects that include clanking equipment, rumbling trucks, zooming aircraft, crashing cannons, and fireworks rocketing through the gathering darkness. They not only provide pleasures in themselves but express the rising excitement manifest in his tone of voice. In print, one can only approximate these effects.

At times throughout his long radio career, he tells the same basic story more than once, his improvisations changing details each time. I've chosen a version that best retains his style and the vivid sense that he is telling the tale in our presence for the first time.

Shepherd occasionally lets slip a sliver of his own history and prejudices, as in his negative allusions toward a decidedly Southern and hillbilly degree of illiteracy in the army he knows. (Working in Cincinnati for a short spell early in his radio career, he lived across the state line in Kentucky and encountered a few country folk.) One notes in some of his original radio renditions his imitation Southern twang and references to towns with disparaging names such as Rabbit Hash and Dismal Seepage.

Shepherd always created intriguingly funny titles for his stories. No funny titles for the new comments and story transcriptions will be found here. I have not attempted to compete with the master.

SOURCES

All the stories in this book were first told on Shep's nightly WOR Radio broadcasts in New York. He did tell army stories earlier, when he was on the air in Cincinnati and Philadelphia, but none have surfaced as audio recordings.

Some stories entered his broadcast audio archives through different sources, occasionally with different names. Some vary slightly in length, through deletion of commercials and other non-Shepherd matter, or through other unknown causes. In general, the army portions of the shows appear complete. No doubt dedicated Shepherd listeners with outstanding memories might have chosen a different Shepherd rendition of a particular story, but any and all improvisations seem worthy of his talent. Many differences between his audio versions are simply courtesy of amateur sound recording, others are thanks to the wonder of Shepherd's improvisational talent.

The various audio archivists labeled their recordings whatever they thought best at the time. Sometimes these titles cite an army story, much of the time not. I've used some of these "original" titles but provided my own where needed.

Dates of broadcasts below match the audio version chosen for the transcription. Some dates are partial, but that's life, until further information comes to light. As for the two undated programs, one is from a syndicated series that was made by cutting extraneous material from a forty-five minute national program.

BROADCAST DATES OF AUDIO VERSIONS SELECTED
[na = NOT AVAILABLE]

PART ONE: YOU'RE IN THE ARMY NOW!

INDUCTION 8/na/1963
SHORN 6/03/1970
"D" IS FOR DRUID 8/13/1973
BEING ORIENTATED........................... 9/03/na
ARMY PHRASEOLOGY .... 1976 or 1977

PART TWO: ARMY HOSPITALITY

SHERMY THE WORMY...................... 9/04/1964
GI GLASSES.................................. 7/10/1965
LIEUTENANT GEORGE L. CHERRY
 TAKES CHARGE 3/31/1972
POLE CLIMBING (complete version
 and a partial version).......... 7/25/1964 and 11/30/1965
SERVICE CLUB VIRTUOSO................... 8/14/1964
FOURTH OF JULY IN THE ARMY 7/03/1963
USO AND A FAMILY INVITATION 11/25/1967
SHIPPING OUT................................. 1969

PART THREE: WARTIME IN FLORIDA IS HELL

MOS: RADAR TECHNICIAN.................. 7/02/1973
RADAR AT FIFTEEN THOUSAND VOLTS........... 1976
SWAMP RADAR.............................. 6/20/1964
NIGHT MANEUVERS............................. 1967
LISTER BAG ATTACK 6/17/1966
BOREDOM ERUPTS 9/18/1969
CODE SCHOOL............... 4/13/1965 and NPR tribute

PART FOUR: AN ARMY EDUCATION: INDEPENDENT STUDY

PART FIVE: MUSTERED OUT AT LAST!

JEAN SHEPHERD AUDIO RESOURCES ON THE WEB:

Schmidco tapes and CDs: www.sheptapes.com

Brassfiglagee.com: www.shepcast.blogspot.com, iTunes, under "podcasts" (originally distributed by the now-defunct Jean Shepherd Project)

www.Insomniatheater.com

Hundreds of Shepherd audios can also be bought from sellers at www.ebay.com.

ACKNOWLEDGMENTS

All books with Jean Shepherd material in them should acknowledge Shepherd for his creative force that reached the level of genius. He's the guilty party.

I thank Kay Radtke, publicist and friend of Jean Shepherd, for picking up on my very conscious-and-not-so-casual-comment to her that a book of Shepherd's army stories would be a great idea. She conveyed the thought to publisher Glenn Young (who also published Shep pals Paddy Chayefsky, Herb Gardner, and Shel Silverstein) whom I also thank. That they are both Shep fans didn't hurt either. My running the idea up the flagpole accompanied by my mental rendition of "Stars and Stripes Forever" resulted in two salutes, and here you have it. Without their friendship and support, who knows how or when this book might ever have been published.

In that regard, for helping speed up the publication process, thank you, Nick Mantis (whose film on Shep is forthcoming), for you know what.

As with any use of Jean Shepherd's broadcasts, thanks must be given to all those who recorded his shows and kept them, and to those who make it their pleasure and business to distribute the programs to the public at large. As always, thank you, Jim Clavin, for maintaining www.flicklives.com, the comprehensive and fantastic site of all things Shepherd, and for your help in locating several army episodes. Of course thank you, Max Schmid, whose WBAI broadcasts and Schmidco, www.sheptapes.com provide a continuing source of Shepherd audios for enjoyment and research.

Thank you, iTunes on the Internet, for the brassfiglagee podcasts of hundreds of Shepherd radio programs, which made my life much simpler and speedier. Most of these iTunes audios originated with Jeff Beauchamp's generous distribution of episodes from his Jean Shepherd Project, sadly no longer extant. Also, regarding the Internet, I couldn't have done it without the research capabilities of www.google.com. Also thanks for the enthusiasm from those in the www.shepgroup@yahoo.com.

As for work on the text of this book, my expert and exacting personal editor, cousin Raymond B. Anderson, has been invaluable.

Not connected with this particular book on Shepherd, but needing acknowledgment in the world of Shep, Manhattan's Paley Center for Media presented a wonderful tribute on January 23, 2012, curated by Ron Simon, "Remembering Master Storyteller, Jean Shepherd." Interviewed by Bill Carter, media reporter for *The New York Times*, Jerry Seinfeld gave extensive evidence as to why he says, "He really formed my entire comedic sensibility. I learned how to do comedy from Jean Shepherd."

Thank you to my wife, Allison Morgan Bergmann, and to our sons, Evan and Drew, long-suffering and bemused family, who continue to live with my Shep-obsessions and who put up with my constant chatter about Shepherd, especially as I often repeat myself. My friends and acquaintances have also aided by lending me their ears. What my listeners may not have realized is that not only do I talk of Shepherd for the pure pleasure of it and the desire to spread the word, but frequently I'm working out an idea that in some form will appear in the book, and the more I construct and reconstruct my verbal essay, the more likely I will find the best means to write it.